MznLnx

Missing Links Exam Preps

Exam Prep for

Managerial Accounting

Hilton, 6th Edition

The MznLnx Exam Prep is your link from the texbook and lecture to your exams.
The MznLnx Exam Preps are unauthorized and comprehensive reviews of your textbooks.

All material provided by MznLnx and Rico Publications (c) 2010
Textbook publishers and textbook authors do not particpate in or contribute to these reviews.

MznLnx

Rico
Publications

Exam Prep for Managerial Accounting
6th Edition
Hilton

Publisher: Raymond Houge
Assistant Editor: Michael Rouger
Text and Cover Designer: Lisa Buckner
Marketing Manager: Sara Swagger
Project Manager, Editorial Production: Jerry Emerson
Art Director: Vernon Lowerui

Product Manager: Dave Mason
Editorial Assitant: Rachel Guzmanji
Pedagogy: Debra Long
Cover Image: Jim Reed/Getty Images
Text and Cover Printer: City Printing, Inc.
Compositor: Media Mix, Inc.

(c) 2010 Rico Publications
ALL RIGHTS RESERVED. No part of this work covered by the copyright may be reproduced or used in any form or by an means--graphic, electronic, or mechanical, including photocopying, recording, taping, Web distribution, information storage, and retrieval systems, or in any other manner--without the written permission of the publisher.

For more information about our products, contact us at:
Dave.Mason@RicoPublications.com

For permission to use material from this text or product, submit a request online to:
Dave.Mason@RicoPublications.com

Printed in the United States
ISBN:

Contents

CHAPTER 1
The Changing Role of Managerial Accounting in a Dynamic Business Environment — 1

CHAPTER 2
Basic Cost Management Concepts and Accounting for Mass Customization Operations — 11

CHAPTER 3
Product Costing and Cost Accumulation in a Batch Production Environment — 18

CHAPTER 4
Process Costing and Hybrid Product-Costing Systems — 24

CHAPTER 5
Activity-Based Costing and Cost Management Systems — 27

CHAPTER 6
Activity-Based Management and Today`s Advanced Manufacturing Environment — 33

CHAPTER 7
Activity Analysis, Cost Behavior, and Cost Estimation — 39

CHAPTER 8
Cost-Volume-Profit Analysis — 44

CHAPTER 9
Profit Planning, Activity-Based Budgeting, and e-Budgeting — 51

CHAPTER 10
Standard Costing, Operational Performance Measures, and the Balanced Scorecard — 58

CHAPTER 11
Flexible Budgeting and the Management of Overhead and Support Activity Costs — 69

CHAPTER 12
Responsibility Accounting, Quality Control, and Environmental Cost Management — 74

CHAPTER 13
Investment Centers and Transfer Pricing — 81

CHAPTER 14
Decision Making; Relevant Costs and Benefits — 93

CHAPTER 15
Target Costing and Cost Analysis for Pricing Decisions — 103

CHAPTER 16
Capital Expenditure Decisions — 111

CHAPTER 17
Absorption, Variable, and Throughput Costing — 121

CHAPTER 18
Allocation of Support Activity Costs and Joint Costs — 125

ANSWER KEY — 134

TO THE STUDENT

COMPREHENSIVE

The *MznLnx* Exam Prep series is designed to help you pass your exams. Editors at MznLnx review your textbooks and then prepare these practice exams to help you master the textbook material. Unlike study guides, workbooks, and practice tests provided by the texbook publisher and textbook authors, *MznLnx* gives you **all** of the material in each chapter in exam form, not just samples, so you can be sure to nail your exam.

MECHANICAL

The MznLnx Exam Prep series creates exams that will help you learn the subject matter as well as test you on your understanding. Each question is designed to help you master the concept. Just working through the exams, you gain an understanding of the subject--its a simple mechanical process that produces success.

INTEGRATED STUDY GUIDE AND REVIEW

MznLnx is not just a set of exams designed to test you, its also a comprehensive review of the subject content. Each exam question is also a review of the concept, making sure that you will get the answer correct without having to go to other sources of material. You learn as you go! Its the easiest way to pass an exam.

HUMOR

Studying can be tedious and dry. MznLnx's instructional design includes moderate humor within the exam questions on occassion, to break the tedium and revitalize the brain

Contents

CHAPTER 1
The Changing Role of Managerial Accounting in a Dynamic Business Environment — 1

CHAPTER 2
Basic Cost Management Concepts and Accounting for Mass Customization Operations — 11

CHAPTER 3
Product Costing and Cost Accumulation in a Batch Production Environment — 18

CHAPTER 4
Process Costing and Hybrid Product-Costing Systems — 24

CHAPTER 5
Activity-Based Costing and Cost Management Systems — 27

CHAPTER 6
Activity-Based Management and Today's Advanced Manufacturing Environment — 33

CHAPTER 7
Activity Analysis, Cost Behavior, and Cost Estimation — 39

CHAPTER 8
Cost-Volume-Profit Analysis — 44

CHAPTER 9
Profit Planning, Activity-Based Budgeting, and e-Budgeting — 51

CHAPTER 10
Standard Costing, Operational Performance Measures, and the Balanced Scorecard — 58

CHAPTER 11
Flexible Budgeting and the Management of Overhead and Support Activity Costs — 69

CHAPTER 12
Responsibility Accounting, Quality Control, and Environmental Cost Management — 74

CHAPTER 13
Investment Centers and Transfer Pricing — 81

CHAPTER 14
Decision Making; Relevant Costs and Benefits — 93

CHAPTER 15
Target Costing and Cost Analysis for Pricing Decisions — 103

CHAPTER 16
Capital Expenditure Decisions — 111

CHAPTER 17
Absorption, Variable, and Throughput Costing — 121

CHAPTER 18
Allocation of Support Activity Costs and Joint Costs — 125

ANSWER KEY — 134

TO THE STUDENT

COMPREHENSIVE

The *MznLnx* Exam Prep series is designed to help you pass your exams. Editors at MznLnx review your textbooks and then prepare these practice exams to help you master the textbook material. Unlike study guides, workbooks, and practice tests provided by the texbook publisher and textbook authors, *MznLnx* gives you **all** of the material in each chapter in exam form, not just samples, so you can be sure to nail your exam.

MECHANICAL

The MznLnx Exam Prep series creates exams that will help you learn the subject matter as well as test you on your understanding. Each question is designed to help you master the concept. Just working through the exams, you gain an understanding of the subject--its a simple mechanical process that produces success.

INTEGRATED STUDY GUIDE AND REVIEW

MznLnx is not just a set of exams designed to test you, its also a comprehensive review of the subject content. Each exam question is also a review of the concept, making sure that you will get the answer correct without having to go to other sources of material. You learn as you go! Its the easiest way to pass an exam.

HUMOR

Studying can be tedious and dry. MznLnx's instructional design includes moderate humor within the exam questions on occassion, to break the tedium and revitalize the brain

Chapter 1. The Changing Role of Managerial Accounting in a Dynamic Business Environment

1. _____ is concerned with the provisions and use of accounting information to managers within organizations, to provide them with the basis to make informed business decisions that will allow them to be better equipped in their management and control functions.

In contrast to financial accountancy information, _____ information is:

- usually confidential and used by management, instead of publicly reported;
- forward-looking, instead of historical;
- pragmatically computed using extensive management information systems and internal controls, instead of complying with accounting standards.

This is because of the different emphasis: _____ information is used within an organization, typically for decision-making.

   a. Governmental accounting
   c. Grenzplankostenrechnung
   b. Management accounting
   d. Nonassurance services

2. A _____ is a type of business entity in which partners (owners) share with each other the profits or losses of the business undertaking in which all have invested. _____s are often favored over corporations for taxation purposes, as the _____ structure does not generally incur a tax on profits before it is distributed to the partners (i.e. there is no dividend tax levied.) However, depending on the _____ structure and the jurisdiction in which it operates, owners of a _____ may be exposed to greater personal liability than they would as shareholders of a corporation.
   a. Corporate governance
   c. National Information Infrastructure Protection Act
   b. Resource Conservation and Recovery Act
   d. Partnership

3. _____ is one of the four Ps of the marketing mix. The other three aspects are product, promotion, and place. It is also a key variable in microeconomic price allocation theory.
   a. Pricing
   c. Price
   b. Target costing
   d. Cost-plus pricing

4. In economics, business, retail, and accounting, a _____ is the value of money that has been used up to produce something, and hence is not available for use anymore. In economics, a _____ is an alternative that is given up as a result of a decision. In business, the _____ may be one of acquisition, in which case the amount of money expended to acquire it is counted as _____.
   a. Cost allocation
   c. Cost
   b. Cost of quality
   d. Prime cost

5. _____ refers to increasing the spiritual, political, social or economic strength of individuals and communities. It often involves the empowered developing confidence in their own capacities.

The term Human _____ covers a vast landscape of meanings, interpretations, definitions and disciplines ranging from psychology and philosophy to the highly commercialized Self-Help industry and Motivational sciences.

   a. IMF
   c. Entity
   b. IPO
   d. Empowerment

Chapter 1. The Changing Role of Managerial Accounting in a Dynamic Business Environment

6. _____ is the process whereby an organization establishes the parameters within which programs, investments, and acquisitions are reaching the desired results. Performance Reference Model of the Federal Enterprise Architecture, 2005.

This process of measuring performance often requires the use of statistical evidence to determine progress toward specific defined organizational objectives.

There are many types of measurements.

 a. Trustee
 b. Management by exception
 c. Management by objectives
 d. Performance measurement

7. _____ is systematic determination of merit, worth, and significance of something or someone using criteria against a set of standards. _____ often is used to characterize and appraise subjects of interest in a wide range of human enterprises, including the arts, criminal justice, foundations and non-profit organizations, government, health care, and other human services.

Depending on the topic of interest, there are professional groups which look to the quality and rigor of the _____ process.

 a. ABC Television Network
 b. AIG
 c. Evaluation
 d. AMEX

8. In economics and sociology, an _____ is any factor (financial or non-financial) that enables or motivates a particular course of action, or counts as a reason for preferring one choice to the alternatives. It is an expectation that encourages people to behave in a certain way. Since human beings are purposeful creatures, the study of _____ structures is central to the study of all economic activity (both in terms of individual decision-making and in terms of co-operation and competition within a larger institutional structure.)

 a. ABC Television Network
 b. AMEX
 c. AIG
 d. Incentive

9. The _____ is a performance management tool which began as a concept for measuring whether the smaller-scale operational activities of a company are aligned with its larger-scale objectives in terms of vision and strategy.

By focusing not only on financial outcomes but also on the operational, marketing and developmental inputs to these, the _____ helps provide a more comprehensive view of a business, which in turn helps organizations act in their best long-term interests. This tool is also being used to address business response to climate change and greenhouse gas emissions.

 a. Balanced scorecard
 b. Best practice
 c. Management by objectives
 d. Trustee

10. _____ is the process of comparing the cost, cycle time, productivity, or quality of a specific process or method to another that is widely considered to be an industry standard or best practice. Essentially, _____ provides a snapshot of the performance of your business and helps you understand where you are in relation to a particular standard. The result is often a business case for making changes in order to make improvements.

Chapter 1. The Changing Role of Managerial Accounting in a Dynamic Business Environment

a. Benchmarking
b. BMC Software, Inc.
c. Strategic business unit
d. 3M Company

11. An _____ is a practitioner of accountancy, which is the measurement, disclosure or provision of assurance about financial information that helps managers, investors, tax authorities and other decision makers make resource allocation decisions.

The word '_____' is derived from the French 'Compter' which took its origin from the Latin 'Computare'. The word was formerly written in English as 'Accomptant', but in process of time the word, which was always pronounced by dropping the 'p', became gradually changed both in pronunciation and in orthography to its present form.

a. AMEX
b. AIG
c. ABC Television Network
d. Accountant

12. The _____ of a company or public agency is the corporate officer primarily responsible for managing the financial risks of the business or agency. This officer is also responsible for financial planning and record-keeping, as well as financial reporting to higher management. (In recent years, however, the role has expanded to encompass communicating financial performance and forecasts to the analyst community.)

a. Merck ' Co., Inc.
b. NASDAQ
c. Chief executive officer
d. Chief financial officer

13. A _____ is a group of employees from various functional areas of the organization - research, engineering, marketing, finance. human resources, and operations, for example - who are all focused on a specific objective and are responsible to work as a team to improve coordination and innovation across divisions and resolve mutual problems.

a. Cross-functional team
b. BNSF Railway
c. 3M Company
d. BMC Software, Inc.

14. An _____ is a term used in behavioral economics to describe those types of behaviors that impose costs on a person in the long-run that are not taken into account when making decisions in the present. Classical Economics discourages government from creating legislation that targets internalities, because it is assumed that the consumer takes these personal costs into account when paying for the good that causes the _____. For example, cigarettes should be taxed because of the negative consumption externalities that they impose, such as second-hand smoke, not because the smoker harms him or herself by smoking.

a. Internality
b. Inventory turnover ratio
c. Operating budget
d. Authorised capital

15. Internal auditing is a profession and activity involved in helping organisations achieve their stated objectives. It does this by utilizing a systematic methodology for analyzing business processes, procedures and activities with the goal of highlighting organizational problems and recommending solutions. Professionals called _____ are employed by organizations to perform the internal auditing activity.

a. Internal auditors
b. Auditor independence
c. Auditing Standards Board
d. Internal Auditing

4   Chapter 1. The Changing Role of Managerial Accounting in a Dynamic Business Environment

16. A _____ is the person responsible for running the treasury of an organization. In A new way to pay the National Debt (1786), James Gillray caricatured Queen Charlotte and George III awash with treasury funds to cover royal debts, with Pitt handing them another moneybag.

The Treasury of a country is the department responsible for the country's economy, finance and revenue. The _____ is generally the head of the Treasury, although, in some countries (such as the U.S. or the UK) the _____ reports to a Secretary of the Treasury, or Chancellor of the Exchequer.

a. BNSF Railway
b. 3M Company
c. BMC Software, Inc.
d. Treasurer

17. _____ describes commerce transactions between businesses, such as between a manufacturer and a wholesaler, or between a wholesaler and a retailer. Contrasting terms are business-to-consumer (B2C) and business-to-government (B2G.)

The volume of B2B transactions is much higher than the volume of B2C transactions.

a. Market share
b. Business-to-business
c. Market segment
d. Value chain

18. _____ is an electronic commerce business model in which consumers (individuals) offer products and services to companies and the companies pay them. This business model is a complete reversal of traditional business model where companies offer goods and services to consumers (business-to-consumer = B2C.)

This kind of economic relationship is qualified as an inverted business type.

a. Redemption value
b. Refunding
c. Consumer-to-business
d. Fund accounting

19. _____, commonly known as e-commerce or eCommerce, consists of the buying and selling of products or services over electronic systems such as the Internet and other computer networks. The amount of trade conducted electronically has grown extraordinarily since the spread of the Internet. A wide variety of commerce is conducted in this way, spurring and drawing on innovations in electronic funds transfer, supply chain management, Internet marketing, online transaction processing, electronic data interchange (EDI), inventory management systems, and automated data collection systems.

a. Electronic data interchange
b. AIG
c. Electronic commerce
d. ABC Television Network

20. _____ is a costing model that identifies activities in an organization and assigns the cost of each activity resource to all products and services according to the actual consumption by each: it assigns more indirect costs (overhead) into direct costs.

In this way an organization can establish the true cost of its individual products and services for the purposes of identifying and eliminating those which are unprofitable and lowering the prices of those which are overpriced.

Chapter 1. The Changing Role of Managerial Accounting in a Dynamic Business Environment 5

In a business organization, the ABC methodology assigns an organization's resource costs through activities to the products and services provided to its customers.

   a. Activity-based costing   b. ABC Television Network
   c. Indirect costs   d. Activity-based management

21. _____ is the application of online and Internet technologies to the business accounting function. Similar to e-mail being an electronic version of traditional mail, _____ is 'electronic enablement' of accounting and accounting processes which are more traditionally manual and paper-based.

_____ involves performing regular accounting functions, accounting research and the accounting training and education through various computer based /internet based accounting tools such as digital tool kits, various internet resources, international web-based materials, institute and company databases which are internet based, web links, internet based accounting software and electronic financial spreadsheet tools to provide efficient decision making.

   a. E-accounting   b. AMEX
   c. AIG   d. ABC Television Network

22. _____ concern the operation of a facility, as opposed to maintenance, supply and distribution, health, and safety, emergency response, human resources, security, information technology and other infrastructural support organizations.

Personnel that make up 'operations' are

- operators
- engineers
- technicians
- management

This is mainly in a manufacturing setting.

   a. Manufacturing operations   b. Trade name
   c. Consolidated financial statements   d. Realization

23. The _____ is one of the three economic sectors, the others being the secondary sector (approximately manufacturing) and the primary sector (extraction such as mining, agriculture and fishing.) Sometimes an additional sector, the 'quaternary sector', is defined for the sharing of information (which normally belongs to the tertiary sector.)

The tertiary sector is defined by exclusion of the two other sectors.

   a. Capital   b. Tertiary sector of economy
   c. Low Income Housing Tax Credit   d. Just-in-time

6 *Chapter 1. The Changing Role of Managerial Accounting in a Dynamic Business Environment*

24. A _____, also client, buyer or purchaser is the buyer or user of the paid products of an individual or organization, mostly called the supplier or seller. This is typically through purchasing or renting goods or services.
    a. 3M Company
    b. BMC Software, Inc.
    c. BNSF Railway
    d. Customer

25. In finance, the _____ between two currencies specifies how much one currency is worth in terms of the other. It is the value of a foreign nation's currency in terms of the home nation's currency. For example an _____ of 102 Japanese yen to the United States dollar means that JPY 102 is worth the same as USD 1.
    a. AIG
    b. AMEX
    c. ABC Television Network
    d. Exchange rate

26. The _____ is a trilateral trade bloc in North America created by the governments of the United States, Canada, and Mexico. The agreement creating the trade bloc came into force on January 1, 1994. It superseded the Canada-United States Free Trade Agreement between the U.S. and Canada.
    a. Collusion
    b. Chief executive officer
    c. Moving average
    d. North American Free Trade Agreement

27. _____ in engineering is a method of manufacturing in which the entire production process is controlled by computer. The traditional separated process methods are joined through a computer by CIM. This integration allows that the processes exchange information with each other and they are able to initiate actions.
    a. BMC Software, Inc.
    b. 3M Company
    c. BNSF Railway
    d. Computer-integrated manufacturing

28. Just in Time could refer to the following:

    - _____, an inventory strategy that reduces in-process inventory
    - _____ compilation, a technique for improving the performance of bytecode-compiled programming systems

    a. Help desk and incident reporting auditing
    b. Fiscal
    c. Comparable
    d. Just-in-time

29. _____ Management is the succession of strategies used by management as a product goes through its _____. The conditions in which a product is sold changes over time and must be managed as it moves through its succession of stages.

    The _____ goes through many phases, involves many professional disciplines, and requires many skills, tools and processes.

    a. Product life cycle
    b. Safety stock
    c. Kaizen
    d. Procurement

30. In commerce, _____ is the length of time it takes from a product being conceived until its being available for sale. _____ is important in industries where products are outmoded quickly. A common assumption is that _____ matters most for first-of-a-kind products, but actually the leader often has the luxury of time, while the clock is clearly running for the followers.

Chapter 1. The Changing Role of Managerial Accounting in a Dynamic Business Environment

a. Procurement
b. Customer satisfaction
c. Kaizen
d. Time to market

31. A _____ is any one of a variety of different systems, institutions, procedures, social relations and infrastructures whereby persons trade, and goods and services are exchanged, forming part of the economy. It is an arrangement that allows buyers and sellers to exchange things. _____s vary in size, range, geographic scale, location, types and variety of human communities, as well as the types of goods and services traded.
a. Perfect competition
b. Market
c. Recession
d. Market Failure

32. _____ is application software that records and processes accounting transactions within functional modules such as accounts payable, accounts receivable, payroll, and trial balance. It functions as an accounting information system. It may be developed in-house by the company or organization using it, may be purchased from a third party, or may be a combination of a third-party application software package with local modifications.
a. AIG
b. Amgen
c. Economic value added
d. Accounting software

33. A _____ is a computer application that simulates a paper worksheet. It displays multiple cells that together make up a grid consisting of rows and columns, each cell containing either alphanumeric text or numeric values. A _____ cell may alternatively contain a formula that defines how the contents of that cell is to be calculated from the contents of any other cell (or combination of cells) each time any cell is updated.
a. Merck ' Co., Inc.
b. Linear regression
c. Mutual fund
d. Spreadsheet

34. _____ Process Deming saw it as part of the 'system' whereby feedback from the process and customer were evaluated against organisational goals.
a. Sensitivity analysis
b. Sole proprietorship
c. Procurement
d. Continuous improvement

35. _____ is the process whereby companies use cost accounting to report or control the various costs of doing business.

The term _____ is widely used in business today. Unfortunately _____ has no uniform definition.

a. Process costing
b. Contribution margin
c. Contribution margin analysis
d. Cost management

36. The International Organization for Standardization (Organisation internationale de normalisation), widely known as _____ , is an international-standard-setting body composed of representatives from various national standards organizations. Founded on 23 February 1947, the organization promulgates worldwide proprietary industrial and commercial standards. It is headquartered in Geneva, Switzerland.
a. AIG
b. AMEX
c. ABC Television Network
d. ISO

8   Chapter 1. The Changing Role of Managerial Accounting in a Dynamic Business Environment

37. _____ is a business management strategy aimed at embedding awareness of quality in all organizational processes. _____ has been widely used in manufacturing, education, call centers, government, and service industries, as well as NASA space and science programs.

When used together as a phrase, the three words in this expression have the following meanings:

- Total: Involving the entire organization, supply chain, and/or product life cycle
- Quality: With its usual definitions, with all its complexities
- Management: The system of managing with steps like Plan, Organize, Control, Lead, Staff, provisioning and organizing.

As defined by the International Organization for Standardization (ISO):

'_____ is a management approach for an organization, centered on quality, based on the participation of all its members and aiming at long-term success through customer satisfaction, and benefits to all members of the organization and to society.' ISO 8402:1994

One major aim is to reduce variation from every process so that greater consistency of effort is obtained. (Royse, D., Thyer, B., Padgett D., ' Logan T., 2006)

In Japan, _____ comprises four process steps, namely:

1. Kaizen - Focuses on 'Continuous Process Improvement', to make processes visible, repeatable and measurable.
2. Atarimae Hinshitsu - The idea that 'things will work as they are supposed to'.
3. Kansei - Examining the way the user applies the product leads to improvement in the product itself.
4. Miryokuteki Hinshitsu - The idea that 'things should have an aesthetic quality' (for example, a pen will write in a way that is pleasing to the writer.)

_____ requires that the company maintain this quality standard in all aspects of its business. This requires ensuring that things are done right the first time and that defects and waste are eliminated from operations.

a. Total quality management
b. BMC Software, Inc.
c. 3M Company
d. BNSF Railway

38. _____ is a method of identifying and evaluating activities that a business performs using activity-based costing to carry out a value chain analysis or a re-engineering initiative to improve strategic and operational decisions in an organization. Activity-based costing establishes relationships between overhead costs and activities so that overhead costs can be more precisely allocated to products, services, or customer segments. _____ focuses on managing activities to reduce costs and improve customer value.

a. Indirect costs
b. ABC Television Network
c. Activity-based costing
d. Activity-based management

39. The _____ is a concept from business management that was first described and popularized by Michael Porter in his 1985 best-seller, Competitive Advantage: Creating and Sustaining Superior Performance.

Chapter 1. The Changing Role of Managerial Accounting in a Dynamic Business Environment

A _____ is a chain of activities. Products pass through all activities of the chain in order and at each activity the product gains some value.

   a. Value chain
   b. Product differentiation
   c. Market segmentation
   d. Customer relationship management

40. _____ is an accounting methodology that traces and accumulates direct costs, and allocates indirect costs of a manufacturing process. Costs are assigned to products, usually in a large batch, which might include an entire month's production. Eventually, costs have to be allocated to individual units of product.
   a. Cost driver
   b. Profit center
   c. Cost management
   d. Process costing

41. _____ is an overall management philosophy introduced by Dr. Eliyahu M. Goldratt in his 1984 book titled The Goal, that is geared to help organizations continually achieve their goal. The title comes from the contention that any manageable system is limited in achieving more of its goal by a very small number of constraints, and that there is always at least one constraint. The _____ process seeks to identify the constraint and restructure the rest of the organization around it, through the use of the Five Focusing Steps.
   a. Lean manufacturing
   b. Six Sigma
   c. Lean production
   d. Theory of constraints

42. The _____ of 2002 (Pub.L. 107-204, 116 Stat. 745, enacted July 30, 2002), also known as the Public Company Accounting Reform and Investor Protection Act of 2002, is a United States federal law enacted on July 30, 2002 in response to a number of major corporate and accounting scandals including those affecting Enron, Tyco International, Adelphia, Peregrine Systems and WorldCom. The legislation establishes new or enhanced standards for all U.S. public company boards, management, and public accounting firms. It does not apply to privately held companies.
   a. Fair Labor Standards Act
   b. FCPA
   c. Lease
   d. Sarbanes-Oxley Act

43. _____ refers to the confirmation of certain characteristics of an object, person, or organization. This confirmation is often, but not always, provided by some form of external review, education, or assessment. One of the most common types of _____ in modern society is professional _____, where a person is certified as being able to competently complete a job or task, usually by the passing of an examination.
   a. BMC Software, Inc.
   b. BNSF Railway
   c. 3M Company
   d. Certification

44. The title _____ is a professional designation awarded by various professional bodies around the world.

The _____ designation is a post-nominal award issued to individuals who have achieved a peer-based criteria of professional competency in the field of Management Accounting. Management accounting qualifications differ from those such as the ACA or CPA 'Chartered' or 'Public' accounting qualifications in a number of ways.

   a. 3M Company
   b. Convey Compliance Systems
   c. BMC Software, Inc.
   d. Certified Management Accountant

Chapter 1. The Changing Role of Managerial Accounting in a Dynamic Business Environment

45. _____, trade certification often called simply certification or qualification, is a designation earned by a person to assure qualification to perform a job or task. Many certifications are used as post-nominal letters indicating an earned privilege from an oversight professional body acting to safeguard the public interest.

Certifications are earned from a Professional society and, in general, must be renewed periodically the life-time of the product upon which the individual is certified.)

a. BNSF Railway
b. 3M Company
c. Professional certification
d. BMC Software, Inc.

46. A _____ is a non-profit organization seeking to further a particular profession, the interests of individuals engaged in that profession, and the public interest.

The roles of these _____s have been variously defined: 'A group of people in a learned occupation who are entrusted with maintaining control or oversight of the legitimate practice of the occupation;' also a body acting 'to safeguard the public interest;' organizations which 'represent the interest of the professional practitioners,' and so 'act to maintain their own privileged and powerful position as a controlling body.'

Such bodies generally strive to achieve a balance between these two often conflicting mandates. Though professional bodies often act to protect the public by maintaining and enforcing standards of training and ethics in their profession, they often also act like a cartel or a labor union for the members of the profession, though this description is commonly rejected by the body concerned.

a. Professional association
b. MicroStrategy
c. HFMA
d. Freddie Mac

Chapter 2. Basic Cost Management Concepts and Accounting for Mass Customization Operations

1. In economics, business, retail, and accounting, a _____ is the value of money that has been used up to produce something, and hence is not available for use anymore. In economics, a _____ is an alternative that is given up as a result of a decision. In business, the _____ may be one of acquisition, in which case the amount of money expended to acquire it is counted as _____.
    a. Cost of quality
    b. Prime cost
    c. Cost allocation
    d. Cost

2. In financial accounting, _____ or cost of sales includes the direct costs attributable to the production of the goods sold by a company. This amount includes the materials cost used in creating the goods along with the direct labor costs used to produce the good. It excludes indirect expenses such as distribution costs and sales force costs.
    a. Reorder point
    b. 3M Company
    c. FIFO and LIFO accounting
    d. Cost of goods sold

3. In accounting, _____ has a very specific meaning. It is an outflow of cash or other valuable assets from a person or company to another person or company. This outflow of cash is generally one side of a trade for products or services that have equal or better current or future value to the buyer than to the seller.
    a. AIG
    b. ABC Television Network
    c. AMEX
    d. Expense

4. _____ is concerned with the provisions and use of accounting information to managers within organizations, to provide them with the basis to make informed business decisions that will allow them to be better equipped in their management and control functions.

In contrast to financial accountancy information, _____ information is:

- usually confidential and used by management, instead of publicly reported;
- forward-looking, instead of historical;
- pragmatically computed using extensive management information systems and internal controls, instead of complying with accounting standards.

This is because of the different emphasis: _____ information is used within an organization, typically for decision-making.

   a. Governmental accounting
   b. Grenzplankostenrechnung
   c. Nonassurance services
   d. Management accounting

5. _____ is one of the four Ps of the marketing mix. The other three aspects are product, promotion, and place. It is also a key variable in microeconomic price allocation theory.
    a. Price
    b. Target costing
    c. Pricing
    d. Cost-plus pricing

6. The phrase _____, according to the Organization for Economic Co-operation and Development, refers to 'creative work undertaken on a systematic basis in order to increase the stock of knowledge, including knowledge of man, culture and society, and the use of this stock of knowledge to devise new applications [sic]'

Chapter 2. Basic Cost Management Concepts and Accounting for Mass Customization Operations

New product design and development is more than often a crucial factor in the survival of a company. In an industry that is fast changing, firms must continually revise their design and range of products. This is necessary due to continuous technology change and development as well as other competitors and the changing preference of customers.

a. BNSF Railway
b. BMC Software, Inc.
c. 3M Company
d. Research and development

7. _____ are formal records of a business' financial activities.

In British English, including United Kingdom company law, _____ are often referred to as accounts, although the term _____ is also used, particularly by accountants.

_____ provide an overview of a business' financial condition in both short and long term.

a. Statement of retained earnings
b. 3M Company
c. Notes to the financial statements
d. Financial statements

8. _____ is a company's financial statement that indicates how the revenue is transformed into the net income The purpose of the _____ is to show managers and investors whether the company made or lost money during the period being reported.

The important thing to remember about an _____ is that it represents a period of time.

a. ABC Television Network
b. AIG
c. AMEX
d. Income statement

9. _____ is a costing model that identifies activities in an organization and assigns the cost of each activity resource to all products and services according to the actual consumption by each: it assigns more indirect costs (overhead) into direct costs.

In this way an organization can establish the true cost of its individual products and services for the purposes of identifying and eliminating those which are unprofitable and lowering the prices of those which are overpriced.

In a business organization, the ABC methodology assigns an organization's resource costs through activities to the products and services provided to its customers.

a. Activity-based management
b. ABC Television Network
c. Indirect costs
d. Activity-based costing

10. In financial accounting, a _____ or statement of financial position is a summary of a person's or organization's balances. Assets, liabilities and ownership equity are listed as of a specific date, such as the end of its financial year. A _____ is often described as a snapshot of a company's financial condition.

Chapter 2. Basic Cost Management Concepts and Accounting for Mass Customization
Operations

a. Financial statements
c. 3M Company
b. Balance sheet
d. Statement of retained earnings

11. _____ concern the operation of a facility, as opposed to maintenance, supply and distribution, health, and safety, emergency response, human resources, security, information technology and other infrastructural support organizations.

Personnel that make up 'operations' are

- operators
- engineers
- technicians
- management

This is mainly in a manufacturing setting.

a. Trade name
c. Consolidated financial statements
b. Manufacturing operations
d. Realization

12. An _____, operating expenditure, operational expense, operational expenditure or OPEX is an on-going cost for running a product, business, or system. Its counterpart, a capital expenditure (CAPEX), is the cost of developing or providing non-consumable parts for the product or system. For example, the purchase of a photocopier is the CAPEX, and the annual paper and toner cost is the OPEX.

a. ABC Television Network
c. AMEX
b. AIG
d. Operating expense

13. In finance, _____ also known as return on investment, rate of profit or sometimes just return, is the ratio of money gained or lost on an investment relative to the amount of money invested. The amount of money gained or lost may be referred to as interest, profit/loss, gain/loss, or net income/loss. The money invested may be referred to as the asset, capital, principal, or the cost basis of the investment.

a. Debt to capital ratio
c. Rate of return
b. Capital employed
d. Theoretical ex-rights price

14. Total _____ is a method of Accounting cost which entails the full cost of manufacturing or providing a service. This includes not just the costs of materials and labour, but also of all manufacturing overheads (whether e;fixede; or e;variablee;.) One of the main reasons for absorbing overheads into the cost of units is for inventory valuation purposes.

a. ABC Television Network
c. AIG
b. AMEX
d. Absorption costing

15. In business and accounting, _____ are everything of value that is owned by a person or company. It is a claim on the property your income of a borrower. The balance sheet of a firm records the monetary value of the _____ owned by the firm.

a. Earnings before interest, taxes, depreciation and amortization
c. Accrual basis accounting
b. Accounts receivable
d. Assets

16. The _____ percentage shows how profitable a company's assets are in generating revenue.

_____ can be computed as:

$$ROA = \frac{\text{Net Income - Interest Expense - Interest Tax savings}}{\text{Average Total Assets}}$$

This number tells you what the company can do with what it has, i.e. how many dollars of earnings they derive from each dollar of assets they control. Its a useful number for comparing competing companies in the same industry.

a. Return on assets
c. Return on sales
b. Capital employed
d. Statutory Liquidity Ratio

17. _____ is the amount of time someone works beyond normal working hours. Normal hours may be determined in several ways:

- by custom (what is considered healthy or reasonable by society),
- by practices of a given trade or profession,
- by legislation,
- by agreement between employers and workers or their representatives.

Most nations have _____ laws designed to dissuade or prevent employers from forcing their employees to work excessively long hours. These laws may take into account other considerations than the humanitarian, such as increasing the overall level of employment in the economy. One common approach to regulating _____ is to require employers to pay workers at a higher hourly rate for _____ work.

a. ABC Television Network
c. Overtime
b. AMEX
d. AIG

18. In business, _____, Overhead cost or _____ expense refers to an ongoing expense of operating a business. The term _____ is usually used to group expenses that are necessary to the continued functioning of the business, but do not directly generate profits.

_____ expenses are all costs on the income statement except for direct labor and direct materials.

a. Intangible assets
c. AIG
b. ABC Television Network
d. Overhead

19. Direct labor and overhead are often called conversion cost while direct material and direct labor are often referred to as _____.

For example, a manufacturing firm pays for raw materials. When activity is decreased, less raw material is used, and so the spending for raw materials falls.

Chapter 2. Basic Cost Management Concepts and Accounting for Mass Customization Operations

a. Marginal cost
b. Cost-volume-profit analysis
c. Cost accounting
d. Prime cost

20. In economics, the _____ is the theory that the price of an object or condition is determined by the sum of the cost of the resources that went into making it. The cost can compose any of the factors of production (including labour, capital, or land) and taxation.

The theory makes the most sense under assumptions of constant returns to scale and the existence of just one non-produced factor of production.

a. BMC Software, Inc.
b. BNSF Railway
c. 3M Company
d. Cost-of-production theory of value

21. The _____ is one of the three economic sectors, the others being the secondary sector (approximately manufacturing) and the primary sector (extraction such as mining, agriculture and fishing.) Sometimes an additional sector, the 'quaternary sector', is defined for the sharing of information (which normally belongs to the tertiary sector.)

The tertiary sector is defined by exclusion of the two other sectors.

a. Capital
b. Just-in-time
c. Low Income Housing Tax Credit
d. Tertiary sector of economy

22. _____s are expenses that change in proportion to the activity of a business. In other words, _____ is the sum of marginal costs. It can also be considered normal costs.

a. Quality costs
b. Fixed costs
c. Cost accounting
d. Variable cost

23. _____ or economic opportunity loss is the value of the next best alternative foregone as the result of making a decision. _____ analysis is an important part of a company's decision-making processes but is not treated as an actual cost in any financial statement. The next best thing that a person can engage in is referred to as the _____ of doing the best thing and ignoring the next best thing to be done.

a. Opportunity cost
b. Inflation
c. AIG
d. ABC Television Network

24. _____ expenses are direct outlays of cash which may or may not be later reimbursed.

In operating a vehicle, gasoline, parking fees and tolls are considered _____ expenses for the trip. Insurance, oil changes, and interest are not, because the outlay of cash covers expenses accrued over a longer period of time.

a. International Financial Reporting Standards
b. AIG
c. Out-of-pocket
d. ABC Television Network

Chapter 2. Basic Cost Management Concepts and Accounting for Mass Customization Operations

25. _____ is subcontracting a process, such as product design or manufacturing, to a third-party company. The decision to outsource is often made in the interest of lowering cost or making better use of time and energy costs, redirecting or conserving energy directed at the competencies of a particular business, or to make more efficient use of land, labor, capital, (information) technology and resources. _____ became part of the business lexicon during the 1980s.

a. US Airways, Inc.
b. USA Today
c. Economic Growth and Tax Relief Reconciliation Act of 2001
d. Outsourcing

26. In economics and business decision-making, _____ are costs that cannot be recovered once they have been incurred. _____ are sometimes contrasted with variable costs, which are the costs that will change due to the proposed course of action, and prospective costs which are costs that will be incurred if an action is taken.

In traditional microeconomic theory, only variable costs are relevant to a decision.

a. Sunk costs
b. BNSF Railway
c. 3M Company
d. BMC Software, Inc.

27. In economics and finance, _____ is the change in total cost that arises when the quantity produced changes by one unit. It is the cost of producing one more unit of a good. Mathematically, the _____ function is expressed as the first derivative of the total cost (TC) function with respect to quantity (Q.)

a. Cost of quality
b. Variable cost
c. Marginal cost
d. Cost accounting

28. Under the average-cost method, it is assumed that the cost of inventory is based on the _____ of the goods available for sale during the period. _____ is computed by dividing the total cost of goods available for sale by the total units available for sale. This gives a weighted-average unit cost that is applied to the units in the ending inventory.

a. Average cost
b. ABC Television Network
c. Ending inventory
d. AIG

29. The _____ of a company or public agency is the corporate officer primarily responsible for managing the financial risks of the business or agency. This officer is also responsible for financial planning and record-keeping, as well as financial reporting to higher management. (In recent years, however, the role has expanded to encompass communicating financial performance and forecasts to the analyst community.)

a. Chief executive officer
b. NASDAQ
c. Chief financial officer
d. Merck ' Co., Inc.

30. _____ refers to an excess amount of information being provided, making processing and absorbing tasks very difficult for the individual because sometimes we cannot see the validity behind the information . As the world moves into a new era of globalization, an increasing number of people are logging onto the internet to conduct their own research and are given the ability to produce as well as consume the data accessed on an increasing number of websites . As of February 2007 there were over 108 million distinct websites and increasing .

a. AIG
b. Information overload
c. ABC Television Network
d. AMEX

Chapter 2. Basic Cost Management Concepts and Accounting for Mass Customization
Operations

31. _____ means the giving out of information, either voluntarily or to be in compliance with legal regulations or workplace rules.

- In Computer security, full _____ means disclosing full information about vulnerabilities.
- In computing, _____ widget
- Journalism, full _____ refers to disclosing the interests of the writer which may bear on the subject being written about, for example, if the writer has worked with an interview subject in the past.

- In law:
    - The law of England and Wales, _____ refers to a process that may form part of legal proceedings, whereby parties inform to other parties the existence of any relevant documents that are, or have been, in their control. This compares with the process known as discovery in the course of legal proceedings in the United States.
    - In U.S. civil procedure (litigation rules for civil cases), _____ is a stage prior to trial. In civil cases, each party must disclose to the opposing party the following: names of witnesses which it may use to support its side, copies of documents (or mere description of these documents) in its control which it may use to support its side, computation of damages claimed, and certain insurance information. _____ is related to, but technically prior to, the discovery stage.
    - In Company law (known as 'corporate law' in the United States), _____ refers to giving out information about public or limited companies or their officers, which might be kept secret if the company was a private company or a partnership.

- In real property transactions, _____ refers to providing to a buyer information known to the seller or broker/agent concerning the condition or other aspects of real property that would affect the property's value or desirability. These rules regarding what information must be disclosed, and whether the information must be disclosed even if a buyer does not ask, vary from one jurisdiction to the next.

a. Trailing
c. Disclosure
b. Tax harmonisation
d. Controlled Foreign Corporations

32. An _____ is a term used in behavioral economics to describe those types of behaviors that impose costs on a person in the long-run that are not taken into account when making decisions in the present. Classical Economics discourages government from creating legislation that targets internalities, because it is assumed that the consumer takes these personal costs into account when paying for the good that causes the _____. For example, cigarettes should be taxed because of the negative consumption externalities that they impose, such as second-hand smoke, not because the smoker harms him or herself by smoking.

a. Internality
c. Authorised capital
b. Inventory turnover ratio
d. Operating budget

Chapter 3. Product Costing and Cost Accumulation in a Batch Production Environment

1. _____ is a costing model that identifies activities in an organization and assigns the cost of each activity resource to all products and services according to the actual consumption by each: it assigns more indirect costs (overhead) into direct costs.

In this way an organization can establish the true cost of its individual products and services for the purposes of identifying and eliminating those which are unprofitable and lowering the prices of those which are overpriced.

In a business organization, the ABC methodology assigns an organization's resource costs through activities to the products and services provided to its customers.

   a. Indirect costs
   b. Activity-based costing
   c. Activity-based management
   d. ABC Television Network

2. _____ are formal records of a business' financial activities.

In British English, including United Kingdom company law, _____ are often referred to as accounts, although the term _____ is also used, particularly by accountants.

_____ provide an overview of a business' financial condition in both short and long term.

   a. Notes to the financial statements
   b. Statement of retained earnings
   c. 3M Company
   d. Financial statements

3. Total _____ is a method of Accounting cost which entails the full cost of manufacturing or providing a service. This includes not just the costs of materials and labour, but also of all manufacturing overheads (whether e;fixede; or e;variablee;.) One of the main reasons for absorbing overheads into the cost of units is for inventory valuation purposes.
   a. AMEX
   b. Absorption costing
   c. ABC Television Network
   d. AIG

4. A _____ has several related meanings:

   - a daily record of events or business; a private _____ is usually referred to as a diary.
   - a newspaper or other periodical, in the literal sense of one published each day;
   - many publications issued at stated intervals, such as magazines, or scholarly academic _____s, or the record of the transactions of a society, are often called _____s. Although _____ is sometimes used, erroneously, as a synonym for 'magazine,' in academic use, a _____ refers to a serious, scholarly publication, most often peer-reviewed. A non-scholarly magazine written for an educated audience about an industry or an area of professional activity is usually called a professional magazine.

The word 'journalist' for one whose business is writing for the public press has been in use since the end of the 17th century.

Open access _____s are scholarly _____s that are available to the reader without financial or other barrier other than access to the internet itself. Some are subsidized, and some require payment on behalf of the author. Subsidized _____s are financed by an academic institution or a government information center.

Chapter 3. Product Costing and Cost Accumulation in a Batch Production Environment   19

a. 3M Company
c. BMC Software, Inc.
b. Journal
d. BNSF Railway

5. The _____ is one of the three economic sectors, the others being the secondary sector (approximately manufacturing) and the primary sector (extraction such as mining, agriculture and fishing.) Sometimes an additional sector, the 'quaternary sector', is defined for the sharing of information (which normally belongs to the tertiary sector.)

The tertiary sector is defined by exclusion of the two other sectors.

a. Capital
c. Low Income Housing Tax Credit
b. Just-in-time
d. Tertiary sector of economy

6. In economics, business, retail, and accounting, a _____ is the value of money that has been used up to produce something, and hence is not available for use anymore. In economics, a _____ is an alternative that is given up as a result of a decision. In business, the _____ may be one of acquisition, in which case the amount of money expended to acquire it is counted as _____.

a. Cost allocation
c. Prime cost
b. Cost of quality
d. Cost

7. In financial accounting, _____ or cost of sales includes the direct costs attributable to the production of the goods sold by a company. This amount includes the materials cost used in creating the goods along with the direct labor costs used to produce the good. It excludes indirect expenses such as distribution costs and sales force costs.

a. 3M Company
c. FIFO and LIFO accounting
b. Cost of goods sold
d. Reorder point

8. _____ concern the operation of a facility, as opposed to maintenance, supply and distribution, health, and safety, emergency response, human resources, security, information technology and other infrastructural support organizations.

Personnel that make up 'operations' are

- operators
- engineers
- technicians
- management

This is mainly in a manufacturing setting.

a. Realization
c. Consolidated financial statements
b. Trade name
d. Manufacturing operations

9. In business, _____, Overhead cost or _____ expense refers to an ongoing expense of operating a business. The term _____ is usually used to group expenses that are necessary to the continued functioning of the business, but do not directly generate profits.

_____ expenses are all costs on the income statement except for direct labor and direct materials.

Chapter 3. Product Costing and Cost Accumulation in a Batch Production Environment

a. ABC Television Network
b. Intangible assets
c. AIG
d. Overhead

10. A _____ is the pinnacle activity involved in selling products or services in return for money or other compensation. It is an act of completion of a commercial activity.

A _____ is completed by the seller, the owner of the goods.

a. Tertiary sector of economy
b. Sale
c. High yield stock
d. Maturity

11. A _____ is an internal document extensively used by projects-based, manufacturing, building and fabrication businesses. A _____ may be for products and/or services. In a manufacturing environment, a _____ is used to signal the start of a manufacturing process and will most probably be linked to a bill of material.

a. Make to order
b. Lean manufacturing
c. Job order
d. Six Sigma

12. A '_____ is the system of organizations, people, technology, activities, information and resources involved in moving a product or service from supplier to customer. _____ activities transform natural resources, raw materials and components into a finished product that is delivered to the end customer. In sophisticated _____ systems, used products may re-enter the _____ at any point where residual value is recyclable.

a. Purchasing
b. Free port
c. Consignor
d. Supply chain

13. _____ is a list of the raw materials, sub-assemblies, intermediate assemblies, sub-components, components, parts and the quantities of each needed to manufacture an end item (final product).

a. Cellular manufacturing
b. Changeover
c. Deming Prize
d. Bill of materials

14. Project _____: The project _____ is a prediction of the costs associated with a particular company project. These costs include labor, materials, and other related expenses. The project _____ is often broken down into specific tasks, with task _____s assigned to each.

a. BNSF Railway
b. Budget
c. 3M Company
d. BMC Software, Inc.

15. _____ refers to the structured transmission of data between organizations by electronic means. It is used to transfer electronic documents from one computer system to another (ie) from one trading partner to another trading partner. It is more than mere E-mail; for instance, organizations might replace bills of lading and even checks with appropriate _____ messages.

a. Electronic commerce
b. AIG
c. ABC Television Network
d. Electronic data interchange

16. A _____ is the rate used to apply manufacturing overhead to work-in-process inventory. It is calculated as estimated manufacturing overhead cost divided by estimated amount of cost driver or activity base. Common activity bases used in the calculation include direct labor costs, direct labor hours, or machine hours.

Chapter 3. Product Costing and Cost Accumulation in a Batch Production Environment 21

    a. Sensitivity analysis
    b. Procurement
    c. Kaizen
    d. Pre-determined overhead rate

17. A '_____' is the unit of an activity that causes the change of an activity cost. A _____ is any activity that causes a cost to be incurred. The Activity Based Costing (ABC) approach relates indirect cost to the activities that drive them to be incurred.
    a. Factory overhead
    b. Contribution margin analysis
    c. Cost driver
    d. Profit center

18. In finance, _____ also known as return on investment, rate of profit or sometimes just return, is the ratio of money gained or lost on an investment relative to the amount of money invested. The amount of money gained or lost may be referred to as interest, profit/loss, gain/loss, or net income/loss. The money invested may be referred to as the asset, capital, principal, or the cost basis of the investment.
    a. Debt to capital ratio
    b. Capital employed
    c. Rate of return
    d. Theoretical ex-rights price

19. In business and accounting, _____ are everything of value that is owned by a person or company. It is a claim on the property your income of a borrower. The balance sheet of a firm records the monetary value of the _____ owned by the firm.
    a. Accounts receivable
    b. Accrual basis accounting
    c. Earnings before interest, taxes, depreciation and amortization
    d. Assets

20. _____ are costs that are not directly accountable to a particular function or product. _____ may be either fixed or variable. _____ include taxes, administration, personnel and security costs, and are also known as overhead.
    a. Activity-based management
    b. ABC Television Network
    c. Activity-based costing
    d. Indirect costs

21. The _____ percentage shows how profitable a company's assets are in generating revenue.

_____ can be computed as:

$$ROA = \frac{\text{Net Income - Interest Expense - Interest Tax savings}}{\text{Average Total Assets}}$$

This number tells you what the company can do with what it has, i.e. how many dollars of earnings they derive from each dollar of assets they control. Its a useful number for comparing competing companies in the same industry.

    a. Capital employed
    b. Return on sales
    c. Statutory Liquidity Ratio
    d. Return on assets

22. The _____ Act 1979 (c.54) is an Act of the Parliament of the United Kingdom which regulates contracts in which goods are sold and bought. The Act consolidates the _____ Act 1893 and subsequent legislation, which in turn consolidated the previous common law.

22 *Chapter 3. Product Costing and Cost Accumulation in a Batch Production Environment*

The _____ Act performs several functions.

a. Sale of goods
c. Municipal bond
b. Social Security Administration
d. Shares authorized

23. _____ is an adverb or adjective, meaning in proportion. The term is used in many legal and economic contexts, and sometimes spelled pro-rata.

More specifically, _____ means:

1. In proportion to some factor that can be exactly calculated.
2. To count based on amount of time that has passed out of the total time.
3. Proportional Ratio

Pro-rata has a Latin etymology, from pro, according to, for, or by, and rata, feminine ablative of calculated .

Examples in law and economics include the following noted below.

a. 3M Company
c. BMC Software, Inc.
b. BNSF Railway
d. Pro rata

24. A _____ rocket is a rocket that uses two or more stages, each of which contains its own engines and propellant. A tandem or serial stage is mounted on top of another stage; a parallel stage is attached alongside another stage. The result is effectively two or more rockets stacked on top of or attached next to each other.

a. BMC Software, Inc.
c. Multistage
b. 3M Company
d. BNSF Railway

25. _____ is a process of attributing cost to particular cost centres. For example the wage of the driver of the purchasing department can be allocated to the purchasing department cost centre. It is not necessary to share the wage cost over several different cost centers.

a. Cost of quality
c. Variable cost
b. Cost allocation
d. Cost accounting

26. _____, commonly known as e-commerce or eCommerce, consists of the buying and selling of products or services over electronic systems such as the Internet and other computer networks. The amount of trade conducted electronically has grown extraordinarily since the spread of the Internet. A wide variety of commerce is conducted in this way, spurring and drawing on innovations in electronic funds transfer, supply chain management, Internet marketing, online transaction processing, electronic data interchange (EDI), inventory management systems, and automated data collection systems.

a. Electronic data interchange
c. AIG
b. ABC Television Network
d. Electronic commerce

27. The term _____ is a term applied to practices that are perfunctory, or seek to satisfy the minimum requirements or to conform to a convention or doctrine. It has different meanings in different fields.

In accounting, _____ earnings are those earnings of companies in addition to actual earnings calculated under the Generally Accepted Accounting Principles (GAAP) in their quarterly and yearly financial reports.

a. Payroll
c. Bottom line

b. Treasury stock
d. Pro forma

Chapter 4. Process Costing and Hybrid Product-Costing Systems

1. _____ is a costing model that identifies activities in an organization and assigns the cost of each activity resource to all products and services according to the actual consumption by each: it assigns more indirect costs (overhead) into direct costs.

In this way an organization can establish the true cost of its individual products and services for the purposes of identifying and eliminating those which are unprofitable and lowering the prices of those which are overpriced.

In a business organization, the ABC methodology assigns an organization's resource costs through activities to the products and services provided to its customers.

    a. Activity-based costing   b. Indirect costs
    c. ABC Television Network   d. Activity-based management

2. _____ concern the operation of a facility, as opposed to maintenance, supply and distribution, health, and safety, emergency response, human resources, security, information technology and other infrastructural support organizations.

Personnel that make up 'operations' are

- operators
- engineers
- technicians
- management

This is mainly in a manufacturing setting.

    a. Consolidated financial statements   b. Trade name
    c. Manufacturing operations   d. Realization

3. In business, _____, Overhead cost or _____ expense refers to an ongoing expense of operating a business. The term _____ is usually used to group expenses that are necessary to the continued functioning of the business, but do not directly generate profits.

_____ expenses are all costs on the income statement except for direct labor and direct materials.

    a. AIG   b. ABC Television Network
    c. Intangible assets   d. Overhead

4. Total _____ is a method of Accounting cost which entails the full cost of manufacturing or providing a service. This includes not just the costs of materials and labour, but also of all manufacturing overheads (whether e;fixede; or e;variablee;.) One of the main reasons for absorbing overheads into the cost of units is for inventory valuation purposes.
    a. AIG   b. AMEX
    c. ABC Television Network   d. Absorption costing

5. In economics, business, retail, and accounting, a _____ is the value of money that has been used up to produce something, and hence is not available for use anymore. In economics, a _____ is an alternative that is given up as a result of a decision. In business, the _____ may be one of acquisition, in which case the amount of money expended to acquire it is counted as _____.

Chapter 4. Process Costing and Hybrid Product-Costing Systems

a. Prime cost
c. Cost of quality
b. Cost allocation
d. Cost

6. A _____ has several related meanings:

- a daily record of events or business; a private _____ is usually referred to as a diary.
- a newspaper or other periodical, in the literal sense of one published each day;
- many publications issued at stated intervals, such as magazines, or scholarly academic _____s, or the record of the transactions of a society, are often called _____s. Although _____ is sometimes used, erroneously, as a synonym for 'magazine,' in academic use, a _____ refers to a serious, scholarly publication, most often peer-reviewed. A non-scholarly magazine written for an educated audience about an industry or an area of professional activity is usually called a professional magazine.

The word 'journalist' for one whose business is writing for the public press has been in use since the end of the 17th century.

Open access _____s are scholarly _____s that are available to the reader without financial or other barrier other than access to the internet itself. Some are subsidized, and some require payment on behalf of the author. Subsidized _____s are financed by an academic institution or a government information center.

a. Journal
c. 3M Company
b. BNSF Railway
d. BMC Software, Inc.

7. In financial accounting, _____ or cost of sales includes the direct costs attributable to the production of the goods sold by a company. This amount includes the materials cost used in creating the goods along with the direct labor costs used to produce the good. It excludes indirect expenses such as distribution costs and sales force costs.

a. 3M Company
c. FIFO and LIFO accounting
b. Cost of goods sold
d. Reorder point

8. _____, in managerial economics is a form of cost accounting. It is a simplified model, useful for elementary instruction and for short-run decisions.

Cost-volume-profit (CVP) analysis expands the use of information provided by breakeven analysis.

a. Fixed costs
c. Cost accounting
b. Cost-volume-profit analysis
d. Cost of quality

9. In economics, and cost accounting, _____ describes the total economic cost of production and is made up of variable costs, which vary according to the quantity of a good produced and include inputs such as labor and raw materials, plus fixed costs, which are independent of the quantity of a good produced and include inputs (capital) that cannot be varied in the short term, such as buildings and machinery. _____ in economics includes the total opportunity cost of each factor of production in addition to fixed and variable costs.

The rate at which _____ changes as the amount produced changes is called marginal cost.

a. BNSF Railway
b. BMC Software, Inc.
c. 3M Company
d. Total cost

10. _____ is the difference between the cost of a good or service and its selling price. A _____ is added on to the total cost incurred by the producer of a good or service in order to create a profit. The total cost reflects the total amount of both fixed and variable expenses to produce and distribute a product.

a. Merck ' Co., Inc.
b. Corporate Bond
c. Statements of Financial Accounting Standards No. 133, Accounting for Derivative Instruments and Hedging Activities
d. Markup

11. _____ is subcontracting a process, such as product design or manufacturing, to a third-party company. The decision to outsource is often made in the interest of lowering cost or making better use of time and energy costs, redirecting or conserving energy directed at the competencies of a particular business, or to make more efficient use of land, labor, capital, (information) technology and resources. _____ became part of the business lexicon during the 1980s.

a. USA Today
b. US Airways, Inc.
c. Economic Growth and Tax Relief Reconciliation Act of 2001
d. Outsourcing

12. A _____ is the rate used to apply manufacturing overhead to work-in-process inventory. It is calculated as estimated manufacturing overhead cost divided by estimated amount of cost driver or activity base. Common activity bases used in the calculation include direct labor costs, direct labor hours, or machine hours.

a. Procurement
b. Sensitivity analysis
c. Kaizen
d. Pre-determined overhead rate

13. A '_____' is the unit of an activity that causes the change of an activity cost. A _____ is any activity that causes a cost to be incurred. The Activity Based Costing (ABC) approach relates indirect cost to the activities that drive them to be incurred.

a. Factory overhead
b. Profit center
c. Contribution margin analysis
d. Cost driver

Chapter 5. Activity-Based Costing and Cost Management Systems

1. _____ is a costing model that identifies activities in an organization and assigns the cost of each activity resource to all products and services according to the actual consumption by each: it assigns more indirect costs (overhead) into direct costs.

In this way an organization can establish the true cost of its individual products and services for the purposes of identifying and eliminating those which are unprofitable and lowering the prices of those which are overpriced.

In a business organization, the ABC methodology assigns an organization's resource costs through activities to the products and services provided to its customers.

   a. ABC Television Network
   b. Activity-based management
   c. Activity-based costing
   d. Indirect costs

2. _____ concern the operation of a facility, as opposed to maintenance, supply and distribution, health, and safety, emergency response, human resources, security, information technology and other infrastructural support organizations.

Personnel that make up 'operations' are

- operators
- engineers
- technicians
- management

This is mainly in a manufacturing setting.

   a. Trade name
   b. Realization
   c. Consolidated financial statements
   d. Manufacturing operations

3. In economics, business, retail, and accounting, a _____ is the value of money that has been used up to produce something, and hence is not available for use anymore. In economics, a _____ is an alternative that is given up as a result of a decision. In business, the _____ may be one of acquisition, in which case the amount of money expended to acquire it is counted as _____.

   a. Prime cost
   b. Cost of quality
   c. Cost allocation
   d. Cost

4. _____ are costs that are not directly accountable to a particular function or product. _____ may be either fixed or variable. _____ include taxes, administration, personnel and security costs, and are also known as overhead.

   a. Activity-based management
   b. ABC Television Network
   c. Indirect costs
   d. Activity-based costing

28 *Chapter 5. Activity-Based Costing and Cost Management Systems*

5. A _____ has several related meanings:

- a daily record of events or business; a private _____ is usually referred to as a diary.
- a newspaper or other periodical, in the literal sense of one published each day;
- many publications issued at stated intervals, such as magazines, or scholarly academic _____s, or the record of the transactions of a society, are often called _____s. Although _____ is sometimes used, erroneously, as a synonym for 'magazine,' in academic use, a _____ refers to a serious, scholarly publication, most often peer-reviewed. A non-scholarly magazine written for an educated audience about an industry or an area of professional activity is usually called a professional magazine.

The word 'journalist' for one whose business is writing for the public press has been in use since the end of the 17th century.

Open access _____s are scholarly _____s that are available to the reader without financial or other barrier other than access to the internet itself. Some are subsidized, and some require payment on behalf of the author. Subsidized _____s are financed by an academic institution or a government information center.

a. 3M Company
b. BMC Software, Inc.
c. BNSF Railway
d. Journal

6. _____ is the balance of the amounts of cash being received and paid by a business during a defined period of time, sometimes tied to a specific project. Measurement of _____ can be used

- to evaluate the state or performance of a business or project.
- to determine problems with liquidity. Being profitable does not necessarily mean being liquid. A company can fail because of a shortage of cash, even while profitable.
- to project rate of returns. The time of _____s into and out of projects are used as inputs to financial models such as internal rate of return, and net present value.
- to examine income or growth of a business when it is believed that accrual accounting concepts do not represent economic realities. Alternately, _____ can be used to 'validate' the net income generated by accrual accounting.

_____ as a generic term may be used differently depending on context, and certain _____ definitions may be adapted by analysts and users for their own uses. Common terms include operating _____ and free _____.

a. Cash flow
b. Controlling interest
c. Commercial paper
d. Flow-through entity

7. _____ is the calculated approximation of a result which is usable even if input data may be incomplete or uncertain.

In statistics, see _____ theory, estimator.

In mathematics, approximation or _____ typically means finding upper or lower bounds of a quantity that cannot readily be computed precisely and is also an educated guess .

Chapter 5. Activity-Based Costing and Cost Management Systems

a. AIG
b. AMEX
c. ABC Television Network
d. Estimation

8. A '_____' is the unit of an activity that causes the change of an activity cost. A _____ is any activity that causes a cost to be incurred. The Activity Based Costing (ABC) approach relates indirect cost to the activities that drive them to be incurred.

a. Profit center
b. Factory overhead
c. Contribution margin analysis
d. Cost driver

9. In business, _____, Overhead cost or _____ expense refers to an ongoing expense of operating a business. The term _____ is usually used to group expenses that are necessary to the continued functioning of the business, but do not directly generate profits.

_____ expenses are all costs on the income statement except for direct labor and direct materials.

a. Overhead
b. AIG
c. Intangible assets
d. ABC Television Network

10. _____ is a common concept in economics, and gives rise to derived concepts such as consumer debt. Generally _____ is defined by opposition to production. But the precise definition can vary because different schools of economists define production quite differently.

a. Yield
b. Starving the beast
c. Mitigating Control
d. Consumption

11. In mathematics _____s are numbers or other things that get multiplied. In particular, see:

- Factorization, the decomposition of an object into a product of other objects
- Integer factorization, the process of breaking down a composite number into smaller non-trivial divisors
- A coefficient
- A divisor of a particular number, or of an element of a monoid
- A von Neumann algebra with a trivial center

In statistics

- _____ analysis is the study of how _____s or certain variables affect variables.

In technology:

- Human _____s, a profession that focuses on how people interact with products, tools, or procedures
- 'Functionality, Application domain, Conditions, Technology, Objects and Responsibility;', In object-oriented programming

Chapter 5. Activity-Based Costing and Cost Management Systems

In computer science and information technology:

- Authentication _____, a piece of information used to verify a person's identity for security purposes
- _____, a Unix command for numbers factorization
- _____ (programming language), an experimental Forth-like programming language

In television:

- The O'Reilly _____, an American talk show hosted by Bill O'Reilly on Fox News.
- The Krypton _____, a British game show hosted by Gordon Burns, formally on ITV. Also had an American version.

a. Valuation
b. Merck ' Co., Inc.
c. The Goodyear Tire ' Rubber Company
d. Factor

12. Homogeneity means 'being similar throughout'.

Homogeneity may also refer to:

- _____, a variety of meanings
- In statistics homogeneity can refer to
    - Homogeneity of variance: Homoscedasticity
    - Logically consistent data matrices: homogeneity (statistics)
- Homogeneity (physics), in physics, two particular meanings: On one hand, translational invariance. On the other, homogeneity of units in equations, related to dimensional analysis
- Homogenetic or homoplastic, in biology, applied both to animals and plants, of having a resemblance in structure, due to descent from a common progenitor with subsequent modification
- Homogenization is intensive mixing of mutually insoluble phases (sometimes with addition of surfactants) to obtain a soluble suspension or emulsion, for example homogenizing milk so that the cream doesn't separate out
- In physical chemistry, _____ describes a single-phase system as opposed to a heterogeneous system. See also phase diagrams and the classification of catalysts
- In the context of procurement/purchasing, _____ is used to describe goods that do not vary in their essential characteristic irrespective of the source of supply

a. Serial bonds
b. Homogeneous
c. Procter ' Gamble
d. Scientific Research and Experimental Development Tax Incentive Program

13. _____ is the process whereby companies use cost accounting to report or control the various costs of doing business.

Chapter 5. Activity-Based Costing and Cost Management Systems

The term _____ is widely used in business today. Unfortunately _____ has no uniform definition.

a. Contribution margin analysis
c. Contribution margin

b. Process costing
d. Cost management

14. _____ is concerned with the provisions and use of accounting information to managers within organizations, to provide them with the basis to make informed business decisions that will allow them to be better equipped in their management and control functions.

In contrast to financial accountancy information, _____ information is:

- usually confidential and used by management, instead of publicly reported;
- forward-looking, instead of historical;
- pragmatically computed using extensive management information systems and internal controls, instead of complying with accounting standards.

This is because of the different emphasis: _____ information is used within an organization, typically for decision-making.

a. Grenzplankostenrechnung
c. Governmental accounting

b. Nonassurance services
d. Management accounting

15. The _____ is a concept from business management that was first described and popularized by Michael Porter in his 1985 best-seller, Competitive Advantage: Creating and Sustaining Superior Performance.

A _____ is a chain of activities. Products pass through all activities of the chain in order and at each activity the product gains some value.

a. Value chain
c. Market segmentation

b. Customer relationship management
d. Product differentiation

16. Closely related to system time is _____, which is a count of the total CPU time consumed by an executing process. It may be split into user and system CPU time, representing the time spent executing user code and system kernel code, respectively. _____s are a tally of CPU instructions or clock cycles and generally have no direct correlation to wall time.

a. Bookkeeping
c. Process time

b. Laffer curve
d. Return on assets

17. The _____ is one of the three economic sectors, the others being the secondary sector (approximately manufacturing) and the primary sector (extraction such as mining, agriculture and fishing.) Sometimes an additional sector, the 'quaternary sector', is defined for the sharing of information (which normally belongs to the tertiary sector.)

The tertiary sector is defined by exclusion of the two other sectors.

a. Tertiary sector of economy
c. Just-in-time
b. Low Income Housing Tax Credit
d. Capital

Chapter 6. Activity-Based Management and Today's Advanced Manufacturing Environment   33

1. A _____ is a manufacturing system in which there is some amount of flexibility that allows the system to react in the case of changes, whether predicted or unpredicted. This flexibility is generally considered to fall into two categories, which both contain numerous subcategories.

The first category, machine flexibility, covers the system's ability to be changed to produce new product types, and ability to change the order of operations executed on a part.

   a. Flexible manufacturing system
   b. BNSF Railway
   c. 3M Company
   d. BMC Software, Inc.

2. Just in Time could refer to the following:

   - _____, an inventory strategy that reduces in-process inventory
   - _____ compilation, a technique for improving the performance of bytecode-compiled programming systems

   a. Help desk and incident reporting auditing
   b. Fiscal
   c. Comparable
   d. Just-in-time

3. _____ is a costing model that identifies activities in an organization and assigns the cost of each activity resource to all products and services according to the actual consumption by each: it assigns more indirect costs (overhead) into direct costs.

In this way an organization can establish the true cost of its individual products and services for the purposes of identifying and eliminating those which are unprofitable and lowering the prices of those which are overpriced.

In a business organization, the ABC methodology assigns an organization's resource costs through activities to the products and services provided to its customers.

   a. Activity-based costing
   b. ABC Television Network
   c. Activity-based management
   d. Indirect costs

4. The International Organization for Standardization (Organisation internationale de normalisation), widely known as _____ , is an international-standard-setting body composed of representatives from various national standards organizations. Founded on 23 February 1947, the organization promulgates worldwide proprietary industrial and commercial standards. It is headquartered in Geneva, Switzerland.
   a. ABC Television Network
   b. AMEX
   c. ISO
   d. AIG

5. _____ is a concept related to lean and just-in-time (JIT) production. The Japanese word _____ is a common everyday term meaning 'signboard' or 'billboard' and utterly lacks the specialized meaning that this loanword has acquired in English. According to Taiichi Ohno, the man credited with developing JIT, _____ is a means through which JIT is achieved.
   a. Kanban
   b. Risk management
   c. FIFO
   d. Trademark

Chapter 6. Activity-Based Management and Today's Advanced Manufacturing Environment

6. In engineering and manufacturing, _____ and quality engineering are used in developing systems to ensure products or services are designed and produced to meet or exceed customer requirements. Refer to the definition by Merriam-Webster for further information. These systems are often developed in conjunction with other business and engineering disciplines using a cross-functional approach.
   a. BMC Software, Inc.
   b. 3M Company
   c. BNSF Railway
   d. Quality control

7. _____ or _____ is a manufacturing philosophy in which the parts having similarities (Geometry, manufacturing process and/or function) are grouped together to achieve higher level of integration between the design and manufacturing functions of a firm.
   a. Lean production
   b. Group technology
   c. Lean manufacturing
   d. Six Sigma

8. _____ refers to a business or organization attempting to acquire goods or services to accomplish the goals of the enterprise. Though there are several organizations that attempt to set standards in the _____ process, processes can vary greatly between organizations. Typically the word e;_____e; is not used interchangeably with the word e;procuremente;, since procurement typically includes Expediting, Supplier Quality, and Traffic and Logistics (T'L) in addition to _____.
   a. Free port
   b. Supply chain
   c. Consignor
   d. Purchasing

9. _____ is a model for workplace design, and is an integral part of lean manufacturing systems. The goal of lean manufacturing is the aggressive minimisation of waste, called muda, to achieve maximum efficiency of resources. _____, sometimes called cellular or cell production, arranges factory floor labor into semi-autonomous and multi-skilled teams, or work cells, who manufacture complete products or complex components.
   a. Changeover
   b. Value engineering
   c. Cellular manufacturing
   d. Productivity

10. _____ in engineering is a method of manufacturing in which the entire production process is controlled by computer. The traditional separated process methods are joined through a computer by CIM. This integration allows that the processes exchange information with each other and they are able to initiate actions.
    a. Computer-integrated manufacturing
    b. BMC Software, Inc.
    c. BNSF Railway
    d. 3M Company

11. _____ concern the operation of a facility, as opposed to maintenance, supply and distribution, health, and safety, emergency response, human resources, security, information technology and other infrastructural support organizations.

Personnel that make up 'operations' are

- operators
- engineers
- technicians
- management

This is mainly in a manufacturing setting.

Chapter 6. Activity-Based Management and Today's Advanced Manufacturing Environment

a. Realization
b. Consolidated financial statements
c. Trade name
d. Manufacturing operations

12. In economics, business, retail, and accounting, a _____ is the value of money that has been used up to produce something, and hence is not available for use anymore. In economics, a _____ is an alternative that is given up as a result of a decision. In business, the _____ may be one of acquisition, in which case the amount of money expended to acquire it is counted as _____.

a. Cost of quality
b. Cost allocation
c. Cost
d. Prime cost

13. _____ is the process whereby companies use cost accounting to report or control the various costs of doing business.

The term _____ is widely used in business today. Unfortunately _____ has no uniform definition.

a. Process costing
b. Contribution margin
c. Contribution margin analysis
d. Cost management

14. _____ are costs that are not directly accountable to a particular function or product. _____ may be either fixed or variable. _____ include taxes, administration, personnel and security costs, and are also known as overhead.

a. Activity-based costing
b. Activity-based management
c. ABC Television Network
d. Indirect costs

15. _____ is a method of identifying and evaluating activities that a business performs using activity-based costing to carry out a value chain analysis or a re-engineering initiative to improve strategic and operational decisions in an organization. Activity-based costing establishes relationships between overhead costs and activities so that overhead costs can be more precisely allocated to products, services, or customer segments. _____ focuses on managing activities to reduce costs and improve customer value.

a. Activity-based costing
b. ABC Television Network
c. Indirect costs
d. Activity-based management

16. _____, in managerial economics is a form of cost accounting. It is a simplified model, useful for elementary instruction and for short-run decisions.

Cost-volume-profit (CVP) analysis expands the use of information provided by breakeven analysis.

a. Fixed costs
b. Cost accounting
c. Cost-volume-profit analysis
d. Cost of quality

17. _____ is the process whereby an organization establishes the parameters within which programs, investments, and acquisitions are reaching the desired results. Performance Reference Model of the Federal Enterprise Architecture, 2005.

This process of measuring performance often requires the use of statistical evidence to determine progress toward specific defined organizational objectives.

Chapter 6. Activity-Based Management and Today's Advanced Manufacturing Environment

There are many types of measurements.

a. Management by exception
b. Management by objectives
c. Trustee
d. Performance measurement

18. _____ is systematic determination of merit, worth, and significance of something or someone using criteria against a set of standards. _____ often is used to characterize and appraise subjects of interest in a wide range of human enterprises, including the arts, criminal justice, foundations and non-profit organizations, government, health care, and other human services.

Depending on the topic of interest, there are professional groups which look to the quality and rigor of the _____ process.

a. ABC Television Network
b. AIG
c. AMEX
d. Evaluation

19. _____ is the process of comparing the cost, cycle time, productivity, or quality of a specific process or method to another that is widely considered to be an industry standard or best practice. Essentially, _____ provides a snapshot of the performance of your business and helps you understand where you are in relation to a particular standard. The result is often a business case for making changes in order to make improvements.

a. BMC Software, Inc.
b. 3M Company
c. Strategic business unit
d. Benchmarking

20. _____ asserts that there is a technique, method, process, activity, incentive or reward that is more effective at delivering a particular outcome than any other technique, method, process, etc. The idea is that with proper processes, checks, and testing, a desired outcome can be delivered with fewer problems and unforeseen complications. _____s can also be defined as the most efficient (least amount of effort) and effective (best results) way of accomplishing a task, based on repeatable procedures that have proven themselves over time for large numbers of people.

a. Performance measurement
b. Management by objectives
c. Cash cow
d. Best practice

21. The term '_____' refers to the concept of collecting information and attempting to spot a pattern in the information. In some fields of study, the term '_____' has more formally-defined meanings.

In project management _____ is a mathematical technique that uses historical results to predict future outcome.

a. 3M Company
b. Multicollinearity
c. Trend analysis
d. Regression analysis

22. _____ Process Deming saw it as part of the 'system' whereby feedback from the process and customer were evaluated against organisational goals.

a. Sensitivity analysis
b. Procurement
c. Continuous improvement
d. Sole proprietorship

Chapter 6. Activity-Based Management and Today's Advanced Manufacturing Environment 37

23. _____ is a pricing method used by firms. It is defined as 'a cost management tool for reducing the overall cost of a product over its entire life-cycle with the help of production, engineering, research and design'. A target cost is the maximum amount of cost that can be incurred on a product and with it the firm can still earn the required profit margin from that product at a particular selling price.
   a. Target costing
   b. Discounts and allowances
   c. Penetration pricing
   d. Pricing

24. Total _____ is a method of Accounting cost which entails the full cost of manufacturing or providing a service. This includes not just the costs of materials and labour, but also of all manufacturing overheads (whether e;fixede; or e;variablee;.) One of the main reasons for absorbing overheads into the cost of units is for inventory valuation purposes.
   a. AMEX
   b. ABC Television Network
   c. AIG
   d. Absorption costing

25. _____ in economics and business is the result of an exchange and from that trade we assign a numerical monetary value to a good, service or asset. If Alice trades Bob 4 apples for an orange, the _____ of an orange is 4 apples. Inversely, the _____ of an apple is 1/4 oranges.
   a. Price
   b. Discounts and allowances
   c. Price discrimination
   d. Transactional Net Margin Method

26. _____ is a Japanese philosophy that focuses on continuous improvement throughout all aspects of life. When applied to the workplace, _____ activities continually improve all functions of a business, from manufacturing to management and from the CEO to the assembly line workers. By improving standardized activities and processes, _____ aims to eliminate waste .
   a. Sensitivity analysis
   b. Proprietorship
   c. Kaizen
   d. Procurement

27. _____ is a systematic method to improve the 'value' of goods or products and services by using an examination of function. Value, as defined, is the ratio of function to cost. Value can therefore be increased by either improving the function or reducing the cost.
   a. Changeover
   b. Productivity
   c. Deming Prize
   d. Value engineering

28. _____ refers to increasing the spiritual, political, social or economic strength of individuals and communities. It often involves the empowered developing confidence in their own capacities.

The term Human _____ covers a vast landscape of meanings, interpretations, definitions and disciplines ranging from psychology and philosophy to the highly commercialized Self-Help industry and Motivational sciences.

   a. IPO
   b. Empowerment
   c. Entity
   d. IMF

29. _____ is an overall management philosophy introduced by Dr. Eliyahu M. Goldratt in his 1984 book titled The Goal, that is geared to help organizations continually achieve their goal. The title comes from the contention that any manageable system is limited in achieving more of its goal by a very small number of constraints, and that there is always at least one constraint. The _____ process seeks to identify the constraint and restructure the rest of the organization around it, through the use of the Five Focusing Steps.

   a. Theory of constraints
   b. Lean production
   c. Six Sigma
   d. Lean manufacturing

Chapter 7. Activity Analysis, Cost Behavior, and Cost Estimation 39

1. In economics, business, retail, and accounting, a _____ is the value of money that has been used up to produce something, and hence is not available for use anymore. In economics, a _____ is an alternative that is given up as a result of a decision. In business, the _____ may be one of acquisition, in which case the amount of money expended to acquire it is counted as _____.

   a. Cost   b. Cost of quality
   c. Cost allocation   d. Prime cost

2. _____ is an area of engineering practice concerned with the 'application of scientific principles and techniques to problems of cost estimating, cost control, business planning and management science, profitability analysis, project management, and planning and scheduling.'

Key objectives of _____ are to arrive at accurate cost estimates and to avoid cost overruns. The broad array of _____ topics represent the intersection of the fields of project management, business management, and engineering. Most people have a limited view of what engineering encompasses.

   a. 3M Company   b. BMC Software, Inc.
   c. BNSF Railway   d. Cost engineering

3. _____ is the calculated approximation of a result which is usable even if input data may be incomplete or uncertain.

In statistics, see _____ theory, estimator.

In mathematics, approximation or _____ typically means finding upper or lower bounds of a quantity that cannot readily be computed precisely and is also an educated guess .

   a. AMEX   b. ABC Television Network
   c. Estimation   d. AIG

4. _____s are expenses that change in proportion to the activity of a business. In other words, _____ is the sum of marginal costs. It can also be considered normal costs.

   a. Cost accounting   b. Variable cost
   c. Fixed costs   d. Quality costs

5. In finance, _____ also known as return on investment, rate of profit or sometimes just return, is the ratio of money gained or lost on an investment relative to the amount of money invested. The amount of money gained or lost may be referred to as interest, profit/loss, gain/loss, or net income/loss. The money invested may be referred to as the asset, capital, principal, or the cost basis of the investment.

   a. Theoretical ex-rights price   b. Capital employed
   c. Rate of return   d. Debt to capital ratio

6. _____, in managerial economics is a form of cost accounting. It is a simplified model, useful for elementary instruction and for short-run decisions.

Cost-volume-profit (CVP) analysis expands the use of information provided by breakeven analysis.

Chapter 7. Activity Analysis, Cost Behavior, and Cost Estimation

a. Fixed costs
b. Cost-volume-profit analysis
c. Cost accounting
d. Cost of quality

7. _____ is a fee paid on borrowed assets. It is the price paid for the use of borrowed money, or, money earned by deposited funds .Assets that are sometimes lent with _____ include money, shares, consumer goods through hire purchase, major assets such as aircraft, and even entire factories in finance lease arrangements. The _____ is calculated upon the value of the assets in the same manner as upon money.

a. Interest
b. ABC Television Network
c. Insolvency
d. AIG

8. An _____ is the price a borrower pays for the use of money they do not own, for instance a small company might borrow from a bank to kick start their business, and the return a lender receives for deferring the use of funds, by lending it to the borrower. _____s are normally expressed as a percentage rate over the period of one year.

_____s targets are also a vital tool of monetary policy and are used to control variables like investment, inflation, and unemployment.

a. AMEX
b. AIG
c. ABC Television Network
d. Interest rate

9. _____ in engineering is a method of manufacturing in which the entire production process is controlled by computer. The traditional separated process methods are joined through a computer by CIM. This integration allows that the processes exchange information with each other and they are able to initiate actions.

a. BMC Software, Inc.
b. Computer-integrated manufacturing
c. BNSF Railway
d. 3M Company

10. A _____ is a manufacturing system in which there is some amount of flexibility that allows the system to react in the case of changes, whether predicted or unpredicted. This flexibility is generally considered to fall into two categories, which both contain numerous subcategories.

The first category, machine flexibility, covers the system's ability to be changed to produce new product types, and ability to change the order of operations executed on a part.

a. Flexible manufacturing system
b. BMC Software, Inc.
c. 3M Company
d. BNSF Railway

11. Just in Time could refer to the following:

- _____, an inventory strategy that reduces in-process inventory
- _____ compilation, a technique for improving the performance of bytecode-compiled programming systems

a. Comparable
b. Help desk and incident reporting auditing
c. Fiscal
d. Just-in-time

Chapter 7. Activity Analysis, Cost Behavior, and Cost Estimation

12. _____ is a costing model that identifies activities in an organization and assigns the cost of each activity resource to all products and services according to the actual consumption by each: it assigns more indirect costs (overhead) into direct costs.

In this way an organization can establish the true cost of its individual products and services for the purposes of identifying and eliminating those which are unprofitable and lowering the prices of those which are overpriced.

In a business organization, the ABC methodology assigns an organization's resource costs through activities to the products and services provided to its customers.

a. ABC Television Network
c. Activity-based management
b. Indirect costs
d. Activity-based costing

13. A '_____' is the unit of an activity that causes the change of an activity cost. A _____ is any activity that causes a cost to be incurred. The Activity Based Costing (ABC) approach relates indirect cost to the activities that drive them to be incurred.

a. Factory overhead
c. Contribution margin analysis
b. Profit center
d. Cost driver

14. In statistics, an _____ is an observation that is numerically distant from the rest of the data.

They can occur by chance in any distribution, but they are often indicative either of measurement error or that the population has a heavy-tailed distribution. In the former case one wishes to discard them or use statistics that are robust to _____s, while in the latter case they indicate that the distribution has high kurtosis and that one should be very cautious in using tool or intuitions that assume a normal distribution.

a. Outlier
c. AMEX
b. ABC Television Network
d. AIG

15. The terms '_____' and 'independent variable' are used in similar but subtly different ways in mathematics and statistics as part of the standard terminology in those subjects. They are used to distinguish between two types of quantities being considered, separating them into those available at the start of a process and those being created by it, where the latter (_____s) are dependent on the former (independent variables.)

In traditional calculus, a function is defined as a relation between two terms called variables because their values vary.

a. BNSF Railway
c. Dependent variable
b. BMC Software, Inc.
d. 3M Company

16. The terms 'dependent variable' and '_____' are used in similar but subtly different ways in mathematics and statistics as part of the standard terminology in those subjects. They are used to distinguish between two types of quantities being considered, separating them into those available at the start of a process and those being created by it, where the latter (dependent variables) are dependent on the former (_____s.)

In traditional calculus, a function is defined as a relation between two terms called variables because their values vary.

a. AIG
b. AMEX
c. ABC Television Network
d. Independent variable

17. The _____ of a statistical model describes how well it fits a set of observations. Measures of _____ typically summarize the discrepancy between observed values and the values expected under the model in question. Such measures can be used in statistical hypothesis testing, e.g. to test for normality of residuals, to test whether two samples are drawn from identical distributions , or whether outcome frequencies follow a specified distribution

a. BMC Software, Inc.
b. BNSF Railway
c. 3M Company
d. Goodness of fit

18. In business, _____, Overhead cost or _____ expense refers to an ongoing expense of operating a business. The term _____ is usually used to group expenses that are necessary to the continued functioning of the business, but do not directly generate profits.

_____ expenses are all costs on the income statement except for direct labor and direct materials.

a. AIG
b. ABC Television Network
c. Overhead
d. Intangible assets

19. Models of the learning curve effect and the closely related _____ effect express the relationship between equations for experience and efficiency or between efficiency gains and investment in the effort. The experience of 'learning curves' was first observed by the 19th Century German psychologist Hermann Ebbinghaus according to the difficulty of memorizing varying numbers of verbal stimuli, and subsequent learning about the complex processes of learning are discussed in the

.

The rule used for representing the learning curve effect states that the more times a task has been performed, the less time will be required on each subsequent iteration.

a. Experience curve
b. ABC Television Network
c. AMEX
d. AIG

20. In economics, _____ is a rise in the general level of prices of goods and services in an economy over a period of time. When the general price level rises, each unit of currency buys fewer goods and services; consequently, _____ is also a decline in the real value of money--a loss of purchasing power in the medium of exchange which is also the monetary unit of account in the economy. A chief measure of general price-level _____ is the general _____ rate, which is the percentage change in a general price index (normally the Consumer Price Index) over time.

a. AIG
b. ABC Television Network
c. Opportunity cost
d. Inflation

Chapter 7. Activity Analysis, Cost Behavior, and Cost Estimation

21. Models of the _____ effect and the closely related experience curve effect express the relationship between equations for experience and efficiency or between efficiency gains and investment in the effort. The experience of '_____s' was first observed by the 19th Century German psychologist Hermann Ebbinghaus according to the difficulty of memorizing varying numbers of verbal stimuli, and subsequent learning about the complex processes of learning are discussed in the

.

The rule used for representing the _____ effect states that the more times a task has been performed, the less time will be required on each subsequent iteration.

   a. Learning curve   b. Strategic business unit
   c. BMC Software, Inc.   d. 3M Company

22. A _____ is a business efficiency technique combining the Time Study work of Frederick Winslow Taylor with the Motion Study work of Frank and Lillian Gilbreth (not to be confused with their son, best known through the biographical 1950 film and book Cheaper by the Dozen.) It is a major part of scientific management (Taylorism.)

A _____ would be used to reduce the number of motions in performing a task in order to increase productivity.

   a. Manufacturing operations   b. Time and motion study
   c. Lump sum   d. Committee on Accounting Procedure

Chapter 8. Cost-Volume-Profit Analysis

1. _____, in managerial economics is a form of cost accounting. It is a simplified model, useful for elementary instruction and for short-run decisions.

Cost-volume-profit (CVP) analysis expands the use of information provided by breakeven analysis.

   a. Cost-volume-profit analysis
   b. Cost accounting
   c. Fixed costs
   d. Cost of quality

2. In accounting, _____ has a very specific meaning. It is an outflow of cash or other valuable assets from a person or company to another person or company. This outflow of cash is generally one side of a trade for products or services that have equal or better current or future value to the buyer than to the seller.
   a. Expense
   b. AMEX
   c. AIG
   d. ABC Television Network

3. An _____, operating expenditure, operational expense, operational expenditure or OPEX is an on-going cost for running a product, business, or system. Its counterpart, a capital expenditure (CAPEX), is the cost of developing or providing non-consumable parts for the product or system. For example, the purchase of a photocopier is the CAPEX, and the annual paper and toner cost is the OPEX.
   a. Operating expense
   b. AMEX
   c. ABC Television Network
   d. AIG

4. In economics ' business, specifically cost accounting, the _____ is the point at which cost or expenses and revenue are equal: there is no net loss or gain, and one has 'broken even'. A profit or a loss has not been made, although opportunity costs have been paid, and capital has received the risk-adjusted, expected return.

For example, if the business sells less than 200 tables each month, it will make a loss, if it sells more, it will be a profit.

   a. BMC Software, Inc.
   b. 3M Company
   c. Defined benefit pension plan
   d. Break-even point

5. In economics, business, retail, and accounting, a _____ is the value of money that has been used up to produce something, and hence is not available for use anymore. In economics, a _____ is an alternative that is given up as a result of a decision. In business, the _____ may be one of acquisition, in which case the amount of money expended to acquire it is counted as _____.
   a. Cost
   b. Cost of quality
   c. Prime cost
   d. Cost allocation

6. In cost-volume-profit analysis, a form of management accounting, _____ is the marginal profit per unit sale. It is a useful quantity in carrying out various calculations, and can be used as a measure of operating leverage.

The Total _____ is Total Revenue (TR, or Sales) minus Total Variable Cost (TVC):

   Tcontribution margin = TR − TVC

Chapter 8. Cost-Volume-Profit Analysis

The Unit _____ (C) is Unit Revenue (Price, P) minus Unit Variable Cost (V):

C = P − V

The _____ Ratio is the percentage of Contribution over Total Revenue, which can be calculated from the unit contribution over unit price or total contribution over Total Revenue:

$$\frac{C}{P} = \frac{P-V}{P} = \frac{\text{Unit Contribution Margin}}{\text{Price}} = \frac{\text{Total Contribution Margin}}{\text{Total Revenue}}$$

For instance, if the price is $10 and the unit variable cost is $2, then the unit _____ is $8, and the _____ ratio is $8/$10 = 80%.

a. Cost management
c. Profit center
b. Factory overhead
d. Contribution margin

7. In business and finance accounting, _____ is equal to the gross profit minus overheads minus interest payable plus/minus one off items for a given time period (usually: accounting period.)

A common synonym for '_____' when discussing financial statements (which include a balance sheet and an income statement) is the bottom line. This term results from the traditional appearance of an income statement which shows all allocated revenues and expenses over a specified time period with the resulting summation on the bottom line of the report.

a. Net profit
c. Cost of goods sold
b. Treasury stock
d. Salvage value

8. A _____ is the pinnacle activity involved in selling products or services in return for money or other compensation. It is an act of completion of a commercial activity.

A _____ is completed by the seller, the owner of the goods.

a. High yield stock
c. Tertiary sector of economy
b. Sale
d. Maturity

9. _____ in economics and business is the result of an exchange and from that trade we assign a numerical monetary value to a good, service or asset. If Alice trades Bob 4 apples for an orange, the _____ of an orange is 4 apples. Inversely, the _____ of an apple is 1/4 oranges.

a. Price
c. Price discrimination
b. Transactional Net Margin Method
d. Discounts and allowances

Chapter 8. Cost-Volume-Profit Analysis

10. An _____ is a comprehensive report on a company's activities throughout the preceding year. _____s are intended to give shareholders and other interested persons information about the company's activities and financial performance. Most jurisdictions require companies to prepare and disclose _____s, and many require the _____ to be filed at the company's registry.

   a. ABC Television Network   b. Annual report
   c. AIG   d. AMEX

11. _____ are formal records of a business' financial activities.

In British English, including United Kingdom company law, _____ are often referred to as accounts, although the term _____ is also used, particularly by accountants.

_____ provide an overview of a business' financial condition in both short and long term.

   a. 3M Company   b. Financial statements
   c. Notes to the financial statements   d. Statement of retained earnings

12. _____ is the study of how the variation (uncertainty) in the output of a mathematical model can be apportioned, qualitatively or quantitatively, to different sources of variation in the input of a model .

In more general terms uncertainty and sensitivity analyses investigate the robustness of a study when the study includes some form of mathematical modelling. While uncertainty analysis studies the overall uncertainty in the conclusions of the study, _____ tries to identify what source of uncertainty weights more on the study's conclusions.

   a. Time to market   b. Free cash flow
   c. Kaizen   d. Sensitivity analysis

13. A _____ is a computer application that simulates a paper worksheet. It displays multiple cells that together make up a grid consisting of rows and columns, each cell containing either alphanumeric text or numeric values. A _____ cell may alternatively contain a formula that defines how the contents of that cell is to be calculated from the contents of any other cell (or combination of cells) each time any cell is updated.

   a. Merck ' Co., Inc.   b. Mutual fund
   c. Linear regression   d. Spreadsheet

14. _____ is a company's financial statement that indicates how the revenue is transformed into the net income The purpose of the _____ is to show managers and investors whether the company made or lost money during the period being reported.

The important thing to remember about an _____ is that it represents a period of time.

   a. ABC Television Network   b. AIG
   c. Income statement   d. AMEX

15. _____, Gross profit margin or Gross Profit Rate can be defined as the amount of contribution to the business enterprise, after paying for direct-fixed and direct-variable unit costs, required to cover overheads (fixed commitments) and provide a buffer for unknown items. It expresses the relationship between gross profit and sales revenue.

It can be expressed in absolute terms:

Gross Profit = Revenue − Cost of Goods Sold

or as the ratio of gross profit to sales revenue, usually in the form of a percentage:

_____ Percentage = (Revenue-Cost of Goods Sold)/Revenue

Cost of goods sold includes variable costs and fixed costs directly linked to the product, such as material and labor.

- a. Gross margin
- c. 3M Company
- b. BMC Software, Inc.
- d. BNSF Railway

16. The _____ is a measure of how revenue growth translates into growth in operating income. It is a measure of leverage, and of how risky (volatile) a company's operating income is.

There are various measures of _____, which can be interpreted analogously to financial leverage.

- a. Upside potential ratio
- c. Operating leverage
- b. Information ratio
- d. AlphaIC

17. In mathematics _____s are numbers or other things that get multiplied. In particular, see:

- Factorization, the decomposition of an object into a product of other objects
- Integer factorization, the process of breaking down a composite number into smaller non-trivial divisors
- A coefficient
- A divisor of a particular number, or of an element of a monoid
- A von Neumann algebra with a trivial center

In statistics

- _____ analysis is the study of how _____s or certain variables affect variables.

In technology:

- Human _____s, a profession that focuses on how people interact with products, tools, or procedures
- 'Functionality, Application domain, Conditions, Technology, Objects and Responsibility;', In object-oriented programming

48 Chapter 8. Cost-Volume-Profit Analysis

In computer science and information technology:

- Authentication _____, a piece of information used to verify a person's identity for security purposes
- _____, a Unix command for numbers factorization
- _____ (programming language), an experimental Forth-like programming language

In television:

- The O'Reilly _____, an American talk show hosted by Bill O'Reilly on Fox News.
- The Krypton _____, a British game show hosted by Gordon Burns, formally on ITV. Also had an American version.

a. The Goodyear Tire ' Rubber Company
b. Factor
c. Merck ' Co., Inc.
d. Valuation

18. Just in Time could refer to the following:

- _____, an inventory strategy that reduces in-process inventory
- _____ compilation, a technique for improving the performance of bytecode-compiled programming systems

a. Fiscal
b. Comparable
c. Help desk and incident reporting auditing
d. Just-in-time

19. _____ is a costing model that identifies activities in an organization and assigns the cost of each activity resource to all products and services according to the actual consumption by each: it assigns more indirect costs (overhead) into direct costs.

In this way an organization can establish the true cost of its individual products and services for the purposes of identifying and eliminating those which are unprofitable and lowering the prices of those which are overpriced.

In a business organization, the ABC methodology assigns an organization's resource costs through activities to the products and services provided to its customers.

a. Activity-based costing
b. Indirect costs
c. ABC Television Network
d. Activity-based management

20. _____ is a term that refers both to:

- a formal discipline used to help appraise, or assess, the case for a project or proposal, which itself is a process known as project appraisal; and
- an informal approach to making decisions of any kind.

Chapter 8. Cost-Volume-Profit Analysis

Under both definitions the process involves, whether explicitly or implicitly, weighing the total expected costs against the total expected benefits of one or more actions in order to choose the best or most profitable option. The formal process is often referred to as either CBA (_____) or BCost-benefit analysis

A hallmark of CBA is that all benefits and all costs are expressed in money terms, and are adjusted for the time value of money, so that all flows of benefits and flows of project costs over time (which tend to occur at different points in time) are expressed on a common basis in terms of their 'e;present value.'e; Closely related, but slightly different, formal techniques include Cost-effectiveness analysis, Economic impact analysis, Fiscal impact analysis and Social Return on Investment(SROI) analysis. The latter builds upon the logic of _____, but differs in that it is explicitly designed to inform the practical decision-making of enterprise managers and investors focused on optimising their social and environmental impacts.

   a. 3M Company
   c. BMC Software, Inc.
   b. Cost-benefit analysis
   d. BNSF Railway

21. The International Organization for Standardization (Organisation internationale de normalisation), widely known as _____ , is an international-standard-setting body composed of representatives from various national standards organizations. Founded on 23 February 1947, the organization promulgates worldwide proprietary industrial and commercial standards. It is headquartered in Geneva, Switzerland.
   a. AMEX
   c. AIG
   b. ABC Television Network
   d. ISO

22. In engineering and manufacturing, _____ and quality engineering are used in developing systems to ensure products or services are designed and produced to meet or exceed customer requirements. Refer to the definition by Merriam-Webster for further information . These systems are often developed in conjunction with other business and engineering disciplines using a cross-functional approach.
   a. BNSF Railway
   c. 3M Company
   b. BMC Software, Inc.
   d. Quality control

23. An _____ is a tax levied on the financial income of people, corporations, or other legal entities. Various _____ systems exist, with varying degrees of tax incidence. Income taxation can be progressive, proportional, or regressive.
   a. Ordinary income
   c. Implied level of government service
   b. Individual Retirement Arrangement
   d. Income tax

24. _____ is equal to the income that a firm has after subtracting costs and expenses from the total revenue. _____ can be distributed among holders of common stock as a dividend or held by the firm as retained earnings.

The items deducted will typically include tax expense, financing expense (interest expense), and minority interest. Likewise, preferred stock dividends will be subtracted too, though they are not an expense.

   a. Matching principle
   c. Long-term liabilities
   b. Net income
   d. Generally accepted accounting principles

25. In physics, and more specifically kinematics, _____ is the change in velocity over time. Because velocity is a vector, it can change in two ways: a change in magnitude and/or a change in direction. In one dimension, _____ is the rate at which something speeds up or slows down.

  a. AMEX
  b. AIG
  c. ABC Television Network
  d. Acceleration

26. _____ refers to any one of several methods by which a company, for 'financial accounting' and/or tax purposes, depreciates a fixed asset in such a way that the amount of depreciation taken each year is higher during the earlier years of an assete;s life. For financial accounting purposes, _____ is generally used when an asset is expected to be much more productive during its early years, so that depreciation expense will more accurately represent how much of an assete;s usefulness is being used up each year. For tax purposes, _____ provides a way of deferring corporate income taxes by reducing taxable income in current years, in exchange for increased taxable income in future years.

  a. Effective marginal tax rates
  b. Accelerated depreciation
  c. User charge
  d. Indirect tax

27. _____ is a term used in accounting, economics and finance to spread the cost of an asset over the span of several years.

In simple words we can say that _____ is the reduction in the value of an asset due to usage, passage of time, wear and tear, technological outdating or obsolescence, depletion, inadequacy, rot, rust, decay or other such factors.

In accounting, _____ is a term used to describe any method of attributing the historical or purchase cost of an asset across its useful life, roughly corresponding to normal wear and tear.

  a. Current asset
  b. Net profit
  c. General ledger
  d. Depreciation

Chapter 9. Profit Planning, Activity-Based Budgeting, and e-Budgeting

1. Project _____: The project _____ is a prediction of the costs associated with a particular company project. These costs include labor, materials, and other related expenses. The project _____ is often broken down into specific tasks, with task _____s assigned to each.

   a. 3M Company
   b. BNSF Railway
   c. BMC Software, Inc.
   d. Budget

2. In economics and sociology, an _____ is any factor (financial or non-financial) that enables or motivates a particular course of action, or counts as a reason for preferring one choice to the alternatives. It is an expectation that encourages people to behave in a certain way. Since human beings are purposeful creatures, the study of _____ structures is central to the study of all economic activity (both in terms of individual decision-making and in terms of co-operation and competition within a larger institutional structure.)

   a. AMEX
   b. ABC Television Network
   c. Incentive
   d. AIG

3. _____ is the process whereby an organization establishes the parameters within which programs, investments, and acquisitions are reaching the desired results. Performance Reference Model of the Federal Enterprise Architecture, 2005.

This process of measuring performance often requires the use of statistical evidence to determine progress toward specific defined organizational objectives.

There are many types of measurements.

   a. Management by objectives
   b. Performance measurement
   c. Trustee
   d. Management by exception

4. _____ is used to assign the available resources in an economic way. It is part of resource management.

In strategic planning, is a plan for using available resources, for example human resources, especially in the near term, to achieve goals for the future.

   a. 3M Company
   b. BMC Software, Inc.
   c. BNSF Railway
   d. Resource allocation

5. _____ is systematic determination of merit, worth, and significance of something or someone using criteria against a set of standards. _____ often is used to characterize and appraise subjects of interest in a wide range of human enterprises, including the arts, criminal justice, foundations and non-profit organizations, government, health care, and other human services.

Depending on the topic of interest, there are professional groups which look to the quality and rigor of the _____ process.

   a. AMEX
   b. Evaluation
   c. ABC Television Network
   d. AIG

6. _____ is a company's financial statement that indicates how the revenue is transformed into the net income The purpose of the _____ is to show managers and investors whether the company made or lost money during the period being reported.

The important thing to remember about an _____ is that it represents a period of time.

a. AIG
b. ABC Television Network
c. AMEX
d. Income statement

7. In business, _____, Overhead cost or _____ expense refers to an ongoing expense of operating a business. The term _____ is usually used to group expenses that are necessary to the continued functioning of the business, but do not directly generate profits.

_____ expenses are all costs on the income statement except for direct labor and direct materials.

a. Intangible assets
b. Overhead
c. AIG
d. ABC Television Network

8. In economics, _____ or _____ goods or real _____ refers to factors of production used to create goods or services that are not themselves significantly consumed (though they may depreciate) in the production process. _____ goods may be acquired with money or financial _____. In finance and accounting, _____ generally refers to financial wealth, especially that used to start or maintain a business.

a. Vyborg Appeal
b. Disclosure
c. Capital
d. Screening

9. _____ is the planning process used to determine whether a firm's long term investments such as new machinery, replacement machinery, new plants, new products, and research development projects are worth pursuing. It is budget for major capital, or investment, expenditures.

Many formal methods are used in _____, including the techniques such as

- Net present value
- Profitability index
- Internal rate of return
- Modified Internal Rate of Return
- Equivalent annuity

These methods use the incremental cash flows from each potential investment, or project. Techniques based on accounting earnings and accounting rules are sometimes used - though economists consider this to be improper - such as the accounting rate of return, and 'return on investment.' Simplified and hybrid methods are used as well, such as payback period and discounted payback period.

a. Capital budgeting
b. Cash flow
c. Preferred stock
d. Gross profit

Chapter 9. Profit Planning, Activity-Based Budgeting, and e-Budgeting

10. _____ are formal records of a business' financial activities.

In British English, including United Kingdom company law, _____ are often referred to as accounts, although the term _____ is also used, particularly by accountants.

_____ provide an overview of a business' financial condition in both short and long term.

a. Statement of retained earnings
b. 3M Company
c. Notes to the financial statements
d. Financial statements

11. A _____ is the pinnacle activity involved in selling products or services in return for money or other compensation. It is an act of completion of a commercial activity.

A _____ is completed by the seller, the owner of the goods.

a. Tertiary sector of economy
b. Maturity
c. High yield stock
d. Sale

12. _____ is the process of estimation in unknown situations. Prediction is a similar, but more general term. Both can refer to estimation of time series, cross-sectional or longitudinal data.

a. 3M Company
b. BMC Software, Inc.
c. Forecasting
d. BNSF Railway

13. The term _____ is a term applied to practices that are perfunctory, or seek to satisfy the minimum requirements or to conform to a convention or doctrine. It has different meanings in different fields.

In accounting, _____ earnings are those earnings of companies in addition to actual earnings calculated under the Generally Accepted Accounting Principles (GAAP) in their quarterly and yearly financial reports.

a. Bottom line
b. Pro forma
c. Payroll
d. Treasury stock

14. _____ is a costing model that identifies activities in an organization and assigns the cost of each activity resource to all products and services according to the actual consumption by each: it assigns more indirect costs (overhead) into direct costs.

In this way an organization can establish the true cost of its individual products and services for the purposes of identifying and eliminating those which are unprofitable and lowering the prices of those which are overpriced.

In a business organization, the ABC methodology assigns an organization's resource costs through activities to the products and services provided to its customers.

a. Activity-based management
b. Indirect costs
c. ABC Television Network
d. Activity-based costing

Chapter 9. Profit Planning, Activity-Based Budgeting, and e-Budgeting

15. _____s are statistical models used in econometrics. An _____ specifies the statistical relationship that is believed to hold between the various economic quantities pertaining a particular economic phenomena under study. An _____ can be derived from a deterministic economic model by allowing for uncertainty or from an economic model which itself is stochastic.

   a. AMEX
                                  b. Econometric model
   c. ABC Television Network
             d. AIG

16. _____ concern the operation of a facility, as opposed to maintenance, supply and distribution, health, and safety, emergency response, human resources, security, information technology and other infrastructural support organizations.

Personnel that make up 'operations' are

- operators
- engineers
- technicians
- management

This is mainly in a manufacturing setting.

   a. Realization
                                  b. Consolidated financial statements
   c. Manufacturing operations
          d. Trade name

17. _____ refers to the methods, practices and operations conducted to promote and sustain certain categories of commercial activity. The term is understood to have different specific meanings depending on the context. Merchandise is a sale goods at a store

In marketing, one of the definitions of _____ is the practice in which the brand or image from one product or service is used to sell another.

   a. 3M Company
                                  b. Merchandise
   c. Merchandising
                               d. BMC Software, Inc.

18. _____ is a demonstration of a process -- such as a variable, term, or object -- relative in terms of the specific process or set of validation tests used to determine its presence and quantity. Properties described in this manner must be sufficiently accessible, so that persons other than the definer may independently measure or test for them at will. An _____ is generally designed to model a conceptual definition.

   a. Operational definition
                       b. AMEX
   c. ABC Television Network
             d. AIG

19. In economics, business, retail, and accounting, a _____ is the value of money that has been used up to produce something, and hence is not available for use anymore. In economics, a _____ is an alternative that is given up as a result of a decision. In business, the _____ may be one of acquisition, in which case the amount of money expended to acquire it is counted as _____.

   a. Cost of quality
                                  b. Cost allocation
   c. Prime cost
                                    d. Cost

Chapter 9. Profit Planning, Activity-Based Budgeting, and e-Budgeting

20. Just in Time could refer to the following:

    - _____, an inventory strategy that reduces in-process inventory
    - _____ compilation, a technique for improving the performance of bytecode-compiled programming systems

    a. Comparable
    c. Just-in-time
    b. Fiscal
    d. Help desk and incident reporting auditing

21. The _____ is one of the three economic sectors, the others being the secondary sector (approximately manufacturing) and the primary sector (extraction such as mining, agriculture and fishing.) Sometimes an additional sector, the 'quaternary sector', is defined for the sharing of information (which normally belongs to the tertiary sector.)

    The tertiary sector is defined by exclusion of the two other sectors.

    a. Just-in-time
    c. Capital
    b. Low Income Housing Tax Credit
    d. Tertiary sector of economy

22. A film _____ determines how much money will be spent on the entire film project. It involves the identification and estimation of cost items for each phase of filmmaking (development, pre-production, production, post-production and distribution.)

    The budget structure is normally split into 'above-the-line' (creative) and 'below-the-line' (technical) costs.

    a. 3M Company
    c. BMC Software, Inc.
    b. BNSF Railway
    d. Production budget

23. _____ refers to a business or organization attempting to acquire goods or services to accomplish the goals of the enterprise. Though there are several organizations that attempt to set standards in the _____ process, processes can vary greatly between organizations. Typically the word e;_____e; is not used interchangeably with the word e;procuremente;, since procurement typically includes Expediting, Supplier Quality, and Traffic and Logistics (T'L) in addition to _____.

    a. Free port
    c. Supply chain
    b. Consignor
    d. Purchasing

24. In accounting, _____ has a very specific meaning. It is an outflow of cash or other valuable assets from a person or company to another person or company. This outflow of cash is generally one side of a trade for products or services that have equal or better current or future value to the buyer than to the seller.

    a. ABC Television Network
    c. AMEX
    b. AIG
    d. Expense

25. In financial accounting, _____ or cost of sales includes the direct costs attributable to the production of the goods sold by a company. This amount includes the materials cost used in creating the goods along with the direct labor costs used to produce the good. It excludes indirect expenses such as distribution costs and sales force costs.

Chapter 9. Profit Planning, Activity-Based Budgeting, and e-Budgeting

a. FIFO and LIFO accounting
b. Cost of goods sold
c. 3M Company
d. Reorder point

26. _____ is the balance of the amounts of cash being received and paid by a business during a defined period of time, sometimes tied to a specific project. Measurement of _____ can be used

- to evaluate the state or performance of a business or project.
- to determine problems with liquidity. Being profitable does not necessarily mean being liquid. A company can fail because of a shortage of cash, even while profitable.
- to project rate of returns. The time of _____s into and out of projects are used as inputs to financial models such as internal rate of return, and net present value.
- to examine income or growth of a business when it is believed that accrual accounting concepts do not represent economic realities. Alternately, _____ can be used to 'validate' the net income generated by accrual accounting.

_____ as a generic term may be used differently depending on context, and certain _____ definitions may be adapted by analysts and users for their own uses. Common terms include operating _____ and free _____.

a. Commercial paper
b. Flow-through entity
c. Controlling interest
d. Cash flow

27. In financial accounting, a _____ or Statement of cash flows is a financial statement that shows a company's flow of cash. The money coming into the business is called cash inflow, and money going out from the business is called cash outflow. The statement shows how changes in balance sheet and income accounts affect cash and cash equivalents, and breaks the analysis down to operating, investing, and financing activities.
a. BMC Software, Inc.
b. 3M Company
c. BNSF Railway
d. Cash flow statement

28. In financial accounting, a _____ or statement of financial position is a summary of a person's or organization's balances. Assets, liabilities and ownership equity are listed as of a specific date, such as the end of its financial year. A _____ is often described as a snapshot of a company's financial condition.
a. 3M Company
b. Balance sheet
c. Financial statements
d. Statement of retained earnings

29. A _____ is a fungible, negotiable instrument representing financial value. they are broadly categorized into debt securities (such as banknotes, bonds and debentures), and equity securities; e.g., common stocks. The company or other entity issuing the _____ is called the issuer.
a. Tracking stock
b. BMC Software, Inc.
c. 3M Company
d. Security

30. _____ is a technique of planning and decision-making which reverses the working process of traditional budgeting. In traditional incremental budgeting, departmental managers justify only increases over the previous year budget and what has been already spent is automatically sanctioned. No reference is made to the previous level of expenditure.
a. BNSF Railway
b. BMC Software, Inc.
c. 3M Company
d. Zero-based budgeting

Chapter 9. Profit Planning, Activity-Based Budgeting, and e-Budgeting

31. _____ Management is the succession of strategies used by management as a product goes through its _____. The conditions in which a product is sold changes over time and must be managed as it moves through its succession of stages.

The _____ goes through many phases, involves many professional disciplines, and requires many skills, tools and processes.

- a. Procurement
- b. Product life cycle
- c. Kaizen
- d. Safety stock

32. In probability theory and statistics, the _____ of a random variable, probability distribution averaging the squared distance of its possible values from the expected value (mean.) Whereas the mean is a way to describe the location of a distribution, the _____ is a way to capture its scale or degree of being spread out. The unit of _____ is the square of the unit of the original variable.
- a. Statistics
- b. Time series
- c. Variance
- d. Monte Carlo methods

33. A _____ is the period of time between the initiation of any process of production and the completion of that process. Thus the _____ for ordering a new car from a manufacturer may be anywhere from 2 weeks to 6 months. In industry, _____ reduction is an important part of lean manufacturing.
- a. 3M Company
- b. Lead time
- c. BNSF Railway
- d. BMC Software, Inc.

34. _____ is a term used by inventory specialists to describe a level of extra stock that is maintained below the cycle stock to buffer against stockouts. _____ exists to counter uncertainties in supply and demand. _____ is defined as extra units of inventory carried as protection against possible stockouts .(shortfall in raw material or packaging.)
- a. Safety stock
- b. Proprietorship
- c. Tax profit
- d. Sensitivity analysis

Chapter 10. Standard Costing, Operational Performance Measures, and the Balanced Scorecard

1. _____ is a 'policy by which management devotes its time to investigating only those situations in which actual results differ significantly from planned results. The idea is that management should spend its valuable time concentrating on the more important items (such as shaping the company's future strategic course.) Attention is given only to material deviations requiring investigation.'

It is not entirely synonymous with the concept of exception management in that it describes a policy where absolute focus is on exception management, in contrast to moderate application of exception management.

   a. Best practice
   b. Cash cow
   c. Performance measurement
   d. Management by exception

2. In economics, business, retail, and accounting, a _____ is the value of money that has been used up to produce something, and hence is not available for use anymore. In economics, a _____ is an alternative that is given up as a result of a decision. In business, the _____ may be one of acquisition, in which case the amount of money expended to acquire it is counted as _____.

   a. Cost allocation
   b. Prime cost
   c. Cost
   d. Cost of quality

3. In probability theory and statistics, the _____ of a random variable, probability distribution averaging the squared distance of its possible values from the expected value (mean.) Whereas the mean is a way to describe the location of a distribution, the _____ is a way to capture its scale or degree of being spread out. The unit of _____ is the square of the unit of the original variable.

   a. Monte Carlo methods
   b. Time series
   c. Statistics
   d. Variance

4. In statistics, _____ (ANOVA) is a collection of statistical models, and their associated procedures, in which the observed variance is partitioned into components due to different explanatory variables. In its simplest form ANOVA gives a statistical test of whether the means of several groups are all equal, and therefore generalizes Student's two-sample t-test to more than two groups.

There are three conceptual classes of such models:

1. Fixed-effects models assumes that the data came from normal populations which may differ only in their means. (Model 1)
2. Random effects models assume that the data describe a hierarchy of different populations whose differences are constrained by the hierarchy. (Model 2)
3. Mixed-effect models describe situations where both fixed and random effects are present. (Model 3)

In practice, there are several types of ANOVA depending on the number of treatments and the way they are applied to the subjects in the experiment:

- One-way ANOVA is used to test for differences among two or more independent groups. Typically, however, the one-way ANOVA is used to test for differences among at least three groups, since the two-group case can be covered by a T-test (Gossett, 1908.)

Chapter 10. Standard Costing, Operational Performance Measures, and the Balanced Scorecard

a. Open database connectivity
b. Intergenerational equity
c. Analysis of variance
d. IMF

5. In accounting, _____ is the original monetary value of an economic item. In some circumstances, assets and liabilities may be shown at their _____, as if there had been no change in value since the date of acquisition. The balance sheet value of the item may therefore differ from the 'true' value.

a. Matching principle
b. Bottom line
c. Historical cost
d. Cost of goods sold

6. _____ is the analysis of how a task is accomplished, including a detailed description of both manual and mental activities, task and element durations, task frequency, task allocation, task complexity, environmental conditions, necessary clothing and equipment, and any other unique factors involved in or required for one or more people to perform a given task. _____ emerged from research in applied behavior analysis and still has considerable research in that area.

Information from a _____ can then be used for many purposes, such as personnel selection and training, tool or equipment design, procedure design (e.g., design of checklists or decision support systems) and automation.

a. 3M Company
b. BMC Software, Inc.
c. BNSF Railway
d. Task analysis

7. _____ is a costing model that identifies activities in an organization and assigns the cost of each activity resource to all products and services according to the actual consumption by each: it assigns more indirect costs (overhead) into direct costs.

In this way an organization can establish the true cost of its individual products and services for the purposes of identifying and eliminating those which are unprofitable and lowering the prices of those which are overpriced.

In a business organization, the ABC methodology assigns an organization's resource costs through activities to the products and services provided to its customers.

a. ABC Television Network
b. Indirect costs
c. Activity-based costing
d. Activity-based management

8. _____ is a concept that denotes the precise probability of specific eventualities. Technically, the notion of _____ is independent from the notion of value and, as such, eventualities may have both beneficial and adverse consequences. However, in general usage the convention is to focus only on potential negative impact to some characteristic of value that may arise from a future event.

a. Risk adjusted return on capital
b. Discounting
c. Discount factor
d. Risk

9. _____ is a concept in economics, finance, and psychology related to the behaviour of consumers and investors under uncertainty. _____ is the reluctance of a person to accept a bargain with an uncertain payoff rather than another bargain with a more certain, but possibly lower, expected payoff. For example, a risk-averse investor might choose to put his or her money into a bank account with a low but guaranteed interest rate, rather than into a stock that is likely to have high returns, but also has a chance of becoming worthless.

Chapter 10. Standard Costing, Operational Performance Measures, and the Balanced Scorecard

a. Risk adjusted return on capital
b. Risk
c. Discount factor
d. Risk aversion

10. Total _____ is a method of Accounting cost which entails the full cost of manufacturing or providing a service. This includes not just the costs of materials and labour, but also of all manufacturing overheads (whether e;fixede; or e;variablee;.) One of the main reasons for absorbing overheads into the cost of units is for inventory valuation purposes.
   a. Absorption costing
   b. AMEX
   c. ABC Television Network
   d. AIG

11. _____ in economics and business is the result of an exchange and from that trade we assign a numerical monetary value to a good, service or asset. If Alice trades Bob 4 apples for an orange, the _____ of an orange is 4 apples. Inversely, the _____ of an apple is 1/4 oranges.
   a. Discounts and allowances
   b. Transactional Net Margin Method
   c. Price discrimination
   d. Price

12. _____ in engineering is a method of manufacturing in which the entire production process is controlled by computer. The traditional separated process methods are joined through a computer by CIM. This integration allows that the processes exchange information with each other and they are able to initiate actions.
   a. BNSF Railway
   b. BMC Software, Inc.
   c. 3M Company
   d. Computer-integrated manufacturing

13. The materials _____ is computed as follows:

   Vmp = (Actual Unit Cost - Standard Unit Cost) * Actual Quantity Purchased

or

   Vmp = (Actual Quantity Purchased * Actual Unit Cost) - (Actual Quantity Purchased * Standard Unit Cost.)

When the Actual Materials Price is higher than the Standard Materials Price, the variance is said to be unfavorable, since the Actual price paid on materials purchased is greater than the allowed standard. The variance is said to be favorable when the Standard materials Price is higher than the Actual Materials Price, since less money was spent in purchasing the materials than the allowed standard.

   a. Price variance
   b. Consolidated financial statements
   c. Fund accounting
   d. Liquidating dividend

14. _____ is an important property of a control system, and the _____ property plays a crucial role in many control problems, such as stabilization of unstable systems by feedback, or optimal control.

_____ and observability are dual aspects of the same problem.

Roughly, the concept of _____ denotes the ability to move a system around in its entire configuration space using only certain admissible manipulations.

Chapter 10. Standard Costing, Operational Performance Measures, and the Balanced Scorecard   61

a. BMC Software, Inc.
c. Controllable

b. Controllability
d. 3M Company

15. A _____ has several related meanings:

- a daily record of events or business; a private _____ is usually referred to as a diary.
- a newspaper or other periodical, in the literal sense of one published each day;
- many publications issued at stated intervals, such as magazines, or scholarly academic _____s, or the record of the transactions of a society, are often called _____s. Although _____ is sometimes used, erroneously, as a synonym for 'magazine,' in academic use, a _____ refers to a serious, scholarly publication, most often peer-reviewed. A non-scholarly magazine written for an educated audience about an industry or an area of professional activity is usually called a professional magazine.

The word 'journalist' for one whose business is writing for the public press has been in use since the end of the 17th century.

Open access _____s are scholarly _____s that are available to the reader without financial or other barrier other than access to the internet itself. Some are subsidized, and some require payment on behalf of the author. Subsidized _____s are financed by an academic institution or a government information center.

a. Journal
c. BNSF Railway

b. BMC Software, Inc.
d. 3M Company

16. Just in Time could refer to the following:

- _____, an inventory strategy that reduces in-process inventory
- _____ compilation, a technique for improving the performance of bytecode-compiled programming systems

a. Comparable
c. Help desk and incident reporting auditing

b. Fiscal
d. Just-in-time

17. _____ is the balance of the amounts of cash being received and paid by a business during a defined period of time, sometimes tied to a specific project. Measurement of _____ can be used

- to evaluate the state or performance of a business or project.
- to determine problems with liquidity. Being profitable does not necessarily mean being liquid. A company can fail because of a shortage of cash, even while profitable.
- to project rate of returns. The time of _____s into and out of projects are used as inputs to financial models such as internal rate of return, and net present value.
- to examine income or growth of a business when it is believed that accrual accounting concepts do not represent economic realities. Alternately, _____ can be used to 'validate' the net income generated by accrual accounting.

_____ as a generic term may be used differently depending on context, and certain _____ definitions may be adapted by analysts and users for their own uses. Common terms include operating _____ and free _____.

Chapter 10. Standard Costing, Operational Performance Measures, and the Balanced Scorecard

a. Controlling interest
c. Cash flow
b. Flow-through entity
d. Commercial paper

18. _____ is the calculated approximation of a result which is usable even if input data may be incomplete or uncertain.

In statistics, see _____ theory, estimator.

In mathematics, approximation or _____ typically means finding upper or lower bounds of a quantity that cannot readily be computed precisely and is also an educated guess .

a. Estimation
c. AMEX
b. ABC Television Network
d. AIG

19. _____ are costs that are not directly accountable to a particular function or product. _____ may be either fixed or variable. _____ include taxes, administration, personnel and security costs, and are also known as overhead.

a. Activity-based costing
c. ABC Television Network
b. Activity-based management
d. Indirect costs

20. In economics, and cost accounting, _____ describes the total economic cost of production and is made up of variable costs, which vary according to the quantity of a good produced and include inputs such as labor and raw materials, plus fixed costs, which are independent of the quantity of a good produced and include inputs (capital) that cannot be varied in the short term, such as buildings and machinery. _____ in economics includes the total opportunity cost of each factor of production in addition to fixed and variable costs.

The rate at which _____ changes as the amount produced changes is called marginal cost.

a. BMC Software, Inc.
c. BNSF Railway
b. Total cost
d. 3M Company

21. _____ is the difference between the cost of a good or service and its selling price. A _____ is added on to the total cost incurred by the producer of a good or service in order to create a profit. The total cost reflects the total amount of both fixed and variable expenses to produce and distribute a product.

a. Corporate Bond
c. Statements of Financial Accounting Standards No. 133, Accounting for Derivative Instruments and Hedging Activities
b. Merck ' Co., Inc.
d. Markup

22. _____ is the state or fact of exclusive rights and control over property, which may be an object, land/real estate or intellectual property. An _____ right is also referred to as title.

_____ is the key building block in the development of the capitalist socio-economic system.

a. Ownership
c. Administrative proceeding
b. ABC Television Network
d. Encumbrance

Chapter 10. Standard Costing, Operational Performance Measures, and the Balanced Scorecard

23. _____ is a financial estimate designed to help consumers and enterprise managers assess direct and indirect costs It is a form of full cost accounting.
    a. BNSF Railway
    b. Total cost of ownership
    c. 3M Company
    d. BMC Software, Inc.

24. Project _____: The project _____ is a prediction of the costs associated with a particular company project. These costs include labor, materials, and other related expenses. The project _____ is often broken down into specific tasks, with task _____s assigned to each.
    a. BNSF Railway
    b. BMC Software, Inc.
    c. 3M Company
    d. Budget

25. A '_____' is the unit of an activity that causes the change of an activity cost. A _____ is any activity that causes a cost to be incurred. The Activity Based Costing (ABC) approach relates indirect cost to the activities that drive them to be incurred.
    a. Cost driver
    b. Profit center
    c. Contribution margin analysis
    d. Factory overhead

26. The International Organization for Standardization (Organisation internationale de normalisation), widely known as _____ , is an international-standard-setting body composed of representatives from various national standards organizations. Founded on 23 February 1947, the organization promulgates worldwide proprietary industrial and commercial standards. It is headquartered in Geneva, Switzerland.
    a. AIG
    b. ISO
    c. ABC Television Network
    d. AMEX

27. In business, _____, Overhead cost or _____ expense refers to an ongoing expense of operating a business. The term _____ is usually used to group expenses that are necessary to the continued functioning of the business, but do not directly generate profits.

    _____ expenses are all costs on the income statement except for direct labor and direct materials.

    a. AIG
    b. ABC Television Network
    c. Intangible assets
    d. Overhead

28. _____ is a business management strategy, initially implemented by Motorola, that today enjoys widespread application in many sectors of industry.

    _____ seeks to improve the quality of process outputs by identifying and removing the causes of defects (errors) and variation in manufacturing and business processes. It uses a set of quality management methods, including statistical methods, and creates a special infrastructure of people within the organization ('Black Belts' etc.)

    a. Lean manufacturing
    b. Make to order
    c. Theory of constraints
    d. Six Sigma

Chapter 10. Standard Costing, Operational Performance Measures, and the Balanced Scorecard

29. In engineering and manufacturing, _____ and quality engineering are used in developing systems to ensure products or services are designed and produced to meet or exceed customer requirements. Refer to the definition by Merriam-Webster for further information . These systems are often developed in conjunction with other business and engineering disciplines using a cross-functional approach.

   a. BMC Software, Inc.
   b. 3M Company
   c. BNSF Railway
   d. Quality control

30. '_____' is Step 7 of 'Philip Crosby's 14 Step Quality Improvement Process' . Although applicable to any type of enterprise, it has been primarily adopted within industry supply chains wherever large volumes of components are being purchased (common items such as nuts and bolts are good examples.)

   _____ was a quality control program originated by the Denver Division of the Martin Marietta Corporation (now Lockheed Martin) on the Titan Missile program, which carried the first astronauts into space in the late 1960s.

   a. BMC Software, Inc.
   b. BNSF Railway
   c. 3M Company
   d. Zero defects

31. _____ is a method of identifying and evaluating activities that a business performs using activity-based costing to carry out a value chain analysis or a re-engineering initiative to improve strategic and operational decisions in an organization. Activity-based costing establishes relationships between overhead costs and activities so that overhead costs can be more precisely allocated to products, services, or customer segments. _____ focuses on managing activities to reduce costs and improve customer value.

   a. ABC Television Network
   b. Activity-based costing
   c. Indirect costs
   d. Activity-based management

32. _____ is the process of comparing the cost, cycle time, productivity, or quality of a specific process or method to another that is widely considered to be an industry standard or best practice. Essentially, _____ provides a snapshot of the performance of your business and helps you understand where you are in relation to a particular standard. The result is often a business case for making changes in order to make improvements.

   a. Strategic business unit
   b. 3M Company
   c. BMC Software, Inc.
   d. Benchmarking

33. _____ is the process whereby an organization establishes the parameters within which programs, investments, and acquisitions are reaching the desired results. Performance Reference Model of the Federal Enterprise Architecture, 2005.

This process of measuring performance often requires the use of statistical evidence to determine progress toward specific defined organizational objectives.

There are many types of measurements.

   a. Trustee
   b. Management by objectives
   c. Management by exception
   d. Performance measurement

Chapter 10. Standard Costing, Operational Performance Measures, and the Balanced Scorecard

34. _____ Management is the succession of strategies used by management as a product goes through its _____. The conditions in which a product is sold changes over time and must be managed as it moves through its succession of stages.

The _____ goes through many phases, involves many professional disciplines, and requires many skills, tools and processes.

   a. Kaizen
   c. Procurement
   b. Safety stock
   d. Product life cycle

35. In finance, _____ also known as return on investment, rate of profit or sometimes just return, is the ratio of money gained or lost on an investment relative to the amount of money invested. The amount of money gained or lost may be referred to as interest, profit/loss, gain/loss, or net income/loss. The money invested may be referred to as the asset, capital, principal, or the cost basis of the investment.

   a. Rate of return
   c. Theoretical ex-rights price
   b. Debt to capital ratio
   d. Capital employed

36. In business and accounting, _____ are everything of value that is owned by a person or company. It is a claim on the property your income of a borrower. The balance sheet of a firm records the monetary value of the _____ owned by the firm.

   a. Accounts receivable
   b. Accrual basis accounting
   c. Earnings before interest, taxes, depreciation and amortization
   d. Assets

37. _____ is systematic determination of merit, worth, and significance of something or someone using criteria against a set of standards. _____ often is used to characterize and appraise subjects of interest in a wide range of human enterprises, including the arts, criminal justice, foundations and non-profit organizations, government, health care, and other human services.

Depending on the topic of interest, there are professional groups which look to the quality and rigor of the _____ process.

   a. ABC Television Network
   c. AMEX
   b. AIG
   d. Evaluation

38. _____ is a demonstration of a process -- such as a variable, term, or object -- relative in terms of the specific process or set of validation tests used to determine its presence and quantity. Properties described in this manner must be sufficiently accessible, so that persons other than the definer may independently measure or test for them at will. An _____ is generally designed to model a conceptual definition.

   a. AIG
   c. ABC Television Network
   b. AMEX
   d. Operational definition

39. The _____ percentage shows how profitable a company's assets are in generating revenue.

Chapter 10. Standard Costing, Operational Performance Measures, and the Balanced Scorecard

_____ can be computed as:

$$ROA = \frac{\text{Net Income - Interest Expense - Interest Tax savings}}{\text{Average Total Assets}}$$

This number tells you what the company can do with what it has, i.e. how many dollars of earnings they derive from each dollar of assets they control. Its a useful number for comparing competing companies in the same industry.

a. Statutory Liquidity Ratio
b. Return on sales
c. Capital employed
d. Return on assets

40. _____ in economics refers to metrics and measures of output from production processes, per unit of input. Labor _____, for example, is typically measured as a ratio of output per labor-hour, an input. _____ may be conceived of as a metrics of the technical or engineering efficiency of production.

a. Cellular manufacturing
b. Productivity
c. Value engineering
d. Deming Prize

41. A _____ is a manufacturing system in which there is some amount of flexibility that allows the system to react in the case of changes, whether predicted or unpredicted. This flexibility is generally considered to fall into two categories, which both contain numerous subcategories.

The first category, machine flexibility, covers the system's ability to be changed to produce new product types, and ability to change the order of operations executed on a part.

a. BMC Software, Inc.
b. 3M Company
c. BNSF Railway
d. Flexible manufacturing system

42. _____ is the process of systematic examination of a quality system carried out by an internal or external quality auditor or an audit team. It is an important part of organization's quality management system and is a key element in the ISO quality system standard, ISO 9001.

_____s are typically performed at predefined time intervals and ensure that the institution has clearly-defined internal quality monitoring procedures linked to effective action.

a. Quality audit
b. 3M Company
c. BNSF Railway
d. BMC Software, Inc.

43. In physics, _____ is defined as the rate of change of position. It is a vector physical quantity; both speed and direction are required to define it. In the SI (metric) system, it is measured in meters per second: (m/s) or ms^{-1}.

a. Job fraud
b. P/E ratio
c. Velocity
d. NASDAQ

Chapter 10. Standard Costing, Operational Performance Measures, and the Balanced Scorecard

44. The general definition of an _____ is an evaluation of a person, organization, system, process, project or product. _____s are performed to ascertain the validity and reliability of information; also to provide an assessment of a system's internal control. The goal of an _____ is to express an opinion on the person/organization/system (etc) in question, under evaluation based on work done on a test basis.

   a. Audit regime
   b. Assurance service
   c. Audit
   d. Institute of Chartered Accountants of India

45. In economics and sociology, an _____ is any factor (financial or non-financial) that enables or motivates a particular course of action, or counts as a reason for preferring one choice to the alternatives. It is an expectation that encourages people to behave in a certain way. Since human beings are purposeful creatures, the study of _____ structures is central to the study of all economic activity (both in terms of individual decision-making and in terms of co-operation and competition within a larger institutional structure.)

   a. Incentive
   b. ABC Television Network
   c. AMEX
   d. AIG

46. The _____ is a performance management tool which began as a concept for measuring whether the smaller-scale operational activities of a company are aligned with its larger-scale objectives in terms of vision and strategy.

   By focusing not only on financial outcomes but also on the operational, marketing and developmental inputs to these, the _____ helps provide a more comprehensive view of a business, which in turn helps organizations act in their best long-term interests. This tool is also being used to address business response to climate change and greenhouse gas emissions.

   a. Best practice
   b. Management by objectives
   c. Trustee
   d. Balanced scorecard

47. _____ is concerned with the provisions and use of accounting information to managers within organizations, to provide them with the basis to make informed business decisions that will allow them to be better equipped in their management and control functions.

   In contrast to financial accountancy information, _____ information is:

   - usually confidential and used by management, instead of publicly reported;
   - forward-looking, instead of historical;
   - pragmatically computed using extensive management information systems and internal controls, instead of complying with accounting standards.

   This is because of the different emphasis: _____ information is used within an organization, typically for decision-making.

   a. Governmental accounting
   b. Nonassurance services
   c. Grenzplankostenrechnung
   d. Management accounting

48. _____ concern the operation of a facility, as opposed to maintenance, supply and distribution, health, and safety, emergency response, human resources, security, information technology and other infrastructural support organizations.

Chapter 10. Standard Costing, Operational Performance Measures, and the Balanced Scorecard

Personnel that make up 'operations' are

- operators
- engineers
- technicians
- management

This is mainly in a manufacturing setting.

a. Consolidated financial statements
c. Trade name

b. Realization
d. Manufacturing operations

Chapter 11. Flexible Budgeting and the Management of Overhead and Support Activity Costs

1. Project _____: The project _____ is a prediction of the costs associated with a particular company project. These costs include labor, materials, and other related expenses. The project _____ is often broken down into specific tasks, with task _____s assigned to each.
    a. 3M Company
    b. BNSF Railway
    c. Budget
    d. BMC Software, Inc.

2. In business, _____, Overhead cost or _____ expense refers to an ongoing expense of operating a business. The term _____ is usually used to group expenses that are necessary to the continued functioning of the business, but do not directly generate profits.

    _____ expenses are all costs on the income statement except for direct labor and direct materials.

    a. Intangible assets
    b. ABC Television Network
    c. AIG
    d. Overhead

3. In economics, business, retail, and accounting, a _____ is the value of money that has been used up to produce something, and hence is not available for use anymore. In economics, a _____ is an alternative that is given up as a result of a decision. In business, the _____ may be one of acquisition, in which case the amount of money expended to acquire it is counted as _____.
    a. Prime cost
    b. Cost of quality
    c. Cost allocation
    d. Cost

4. _____ in engineering is a method of manufacturing in which the entire production process is controlled by computer. The traditional separated process methods are joined through a computer by CIM. This integration allows that the processes exchange information with each other and they are able to initiate actions.
    a. BNSF Railway
    b. 3M Company
    c. Computer-integrated manufacturing
    d. BMC Software, Inc.

5. Just in Time could refer to the following:

    - _____, an inventory strategy that reduces in-process inventory
    - _____ compilation, a technique for improving the performance of bytecode-compiled programming systems

    a. Comparable
    b. Fiscal
    c. Help desk and incident reporting auditing
    d. Just-in-time

6. _____ is a costing model that identifies activities in an organization and assigns the cost of each activity resource to all products and services according to the actual consumption by each: it assigns more indirect costs (overhead) into direct costs.

In this way an organization can establish the true cost of its individual products and services for the purposes of identifying and eliminating those which are unprofitable and lowering the prices of those which are overpriced.

In a business organization, the ABC methodology assigns an organization's resource costs through activities to the products and services provided to its customers.

Chapter 11. Flexible Budgeting and the Management of Overhead and Support Activity Costs

    a. Indirect costs
    b. Activity-based management
    c. Activity-based costing
    d. ABC Television Network

7. A '_____' is the unit of an activity that causes the change of an activity cost. A _____ is any activity that causes a cost to be incurred. The Activity Based Costing (ABC) approach relates indirect cost to the activities that drive them to be incurred.
    a. Factory overhead
    b. Cost driver
    c. Contribution margin analysis
    d. Profit center

8. _____ is the process whereby companies use cost accounting to report or control the various costs of doing business.

The term _____ is widely used in business today. Unfortunately _____ has no uniform definition.

    a. Contribution margin
    b. Process costing
    c. Contribution margin analysis
    d. Cost management

9. _____ are costs that are not directly accountable to a particular function or product. _____ may be either fixed or variable. _____ include taxes, administration, personnel and security costs, and are also known as overhead.
    a. Activity-based costing
    b. Activity-based management
    c. ABC Television Network
    d. Indirect costs

10. In probability theory and statistics, the _____ of a random variable, probability distribution averaging the squared distance of its possible values from the expected value (mean.) Whereas the mean is a way to describe the location of a distribution, the _____ is a way to capture its scale or degree of being spread out. The unit of _____ is the square of the unit of the original variable.
    a. Time series
    b. Statistics
    c. Monte Carlo methods
    d. Variance

11. In statistics, _____ (ANOVA) is a collection of statistical models, and their associated procedures, in which the observed variance is partitioned into components due to different explanatory variables. In its simplest form ANOVA gives a statistical test of whether the means of several groups are all equal, and therefore generalizes Student's two-sample t-test to more than two groups.

There are three conceptual classes of such models:

1. Fixed-effects models assumes that the data came from normal populations which may differ only in their means. (Model 1)
2. Random effects models assume that the data describe a hierarchy of different populations whose differences are constrained by the hierarchy. (Model 2)
3. Mixed-effect models describe situations where both fixed and random effects are present. (Model 3)

Chapter 11. Flexible Budgeting and the Management of Overhead and Support Activity Costs

In practice, there are several types of ANOVA depending on the number of treatments and the way they are applied to the subjects in the experiment:

- One-way ANOVA is used to test for differences among two or more independent groups. Typically, however, the one-way ANOVA is used to test for differences among at least three groups, since the two-group case can be covered by a T-test (Gossett, 1908.)

   a. Analysis of variance   b. Open database connectivity
   c. Intergenerational equity   d. IMF

12. _____ is a common concept in economics, and gives rise to derived concepts such as consumer debt. Generally _____ is defined by opposition to production. But the precise definition can vary because different schools of economists define production quite differently.

   a. Mitigating Control   b. Starving the beast
   c. Yield   d. Consumption

13. _____ is a concept in economics which refers to the extent to which an enterprise or a nation actually uses its installed productive capacity. Thus, it refers to the relationship between actual output that 'is' produced with the installed equipment and the potential output which 'could' be produced with it, if capacity was fully used.

If market demand grows, _____ will rise.

   a. BMC Software, Inc.   b. Capacity utilization
   c. Long-run   d. 3M Company

14. Government _____ are designed to show nonfinancial aspects of government operations. For example, a government financial report might include the number of arrests, number of convictions by crime category as well as the change (i.e., increase or decrease) in crime rate. Government _____ usually provide data on environmental conditions, education and conditions of streets and roads.

   a. BMC Software, Inc.   b. 3M Company
   c. BNSF Railway   d. Performance reports

15. _____ is the process whereby an organization establishes the parameters within which programs, investments, and acquisitions are reaching the desired results. Performance Reference Model of the Federal Enterprise Architecture, 2005.

This process of measuring performance often requires the use of statistical evidence to determine progress toward specific defined organizational objectives.

There are many types of measurements.

   a. Management by exception   b. Performance measurement
   c. Trustee   d. Management by objectives

Chapter 11. Flexible Budgeting and the Management of Overhead and Support Activity Costs

16. _____ is systematic determination of merit, worth, and significance of something or someone using criteria against a set of standards. _____ often is used to characterize and appraise subjects of interest in a wide range of human enterprises, including the arts, criminal justice, foundations and non-profit organizations, government, health care, and other human services.

Depending on the topic of interest, there are professional groups which look to the quality and rigor of the _____ process.

    a. AMEX   b. Evaluation
    c. ABC Television Network   d. AIG

17. A _____ has several related meanings:

- a daily record of events or business; a private _____ is usually referred to as a diary.
- a newspaper or other periodical, in the literal sense of one published each day;
- many publications issued at stated intervals, such as magazines, or scholarly academic _____s, or the record of the transactions of a society, are often called _____s. Although _____ is sometimes used, erroneously, as a synonym for 'magazine,' in academic use, a _____ refers to a serious, scholarly publication, most often peer-reviewed. A non-scholarly magazine written for an educated audience about an industry or an area of professional activity is usually called a professional magazine.

The word 'journalist' for one whose business is writing for the public press has been in use since the end of the 17th century.

Open access _____s are scholarly _____s that are available to the reader without financial or other barrier other than access to the internet itself. Some are subsidized, and some require payment on behalf of the author. Subsidized _____s are financed by an academic institution or a government information center.

    a. BNSF Railway   b. BMC Software, Inc.
    c. Journal   d. 3M Company

18. A _____ is the pinnacle activity involved in selling products or services in return for money or other compensation. It is an act of completion of a commercial activity.

A _____ is completed by the seller, the owner of the goods.

    a. Tertiary sector of economy   b. Maturity
    c. High yield stock   d. Sale

19. In cost-volume-profit analysis, a form of management accounting, _____ is the marginal profit per unit sale. It is a useful quantity in carrying out various calculations, and can be used as a measure of operating leverage.

Chapter 11. Flexible Budgeting and the Management of Overhead and Support Activity Costs

The Total _____ is Total Revenue (TR, or Sales) minus Total Variable Cost (TVC):

Tcontribution margin = TR − TVC

The Unit _____ (C) is Unit Revenue (Price, P) minus Unit Variable Cost (V):

C = P − V

The _____ Ratio is the percentage of Contribution over Total Revenue, which can be calculated from the unit contribution over unit price or total contribution over Total Revenue:

$$\frac{C}{P} = \frac{P-V}{P} = \frac{\text{Unit Contribution Margin}}{\text{Price}} = \frac{\text{Total Contribution Margin}}{\text{Total Revenue}}$$

For instance, if the price is $10 and the unit variable cost is $2, then the unit _____ is $8, and the _____ ratio is $8/$10 = 80%.

a. Contribution margin
c. Factory overhead
b. Cost management
d. Profit center

Chapter 12. Responsibility Accounting, Quality Control, and Environmental Cost Management

1. In economics, business, retail, and accounting, a _____ is the value of money that has been used up to produce something, and hence is not available for use anymore. In economics, a _____ is an alternative that is given up as a result of a decision. In business, the _____ may be one of acquisition, in which case the amount of money expended to acquire it is counted as _____.
   a. Cost allocation
   b. Cost of quality
   c. Prime cost
   d. Cost

2. An _____ is a classification used for business units within an enterprise. The essential element of an _____ is that it is treated as a unit which is measured against its use of capital, as opposed to a cost or profit center, which are measured against raw costs or profits.

   The advantage of this form of measurement is that it tends to be more encompassing, since it accounts for all uses of capital.

   a. AIG
   b. ABC Television Network
   c. AMEX
   d. Investment center

3. _____s are parts of a corporation that directly add to its profit.

   A _____ manager is held accountable for both revenues, and costs (expenses), and therefore, profits. What this means in terms of managerial responsibilities is that the manager has to drive the sales revenue generating activities which leads to cash inflows and at the same time control the cost (cash outflows) causing activities.

   a. Contribution margin
   b. Cost management
   c. Profit center
   d. Cost driver

4. _____ is a 'policy by which management devotes its time to investigating only those situations in which actual results differ significantly from planned results. The idea is that management should spend its valuable time concentrating on the more important items (such as shaping the company's future strategic course.) Attention is given only to material deviations requiring investigation.'

   It is not entirely synonymous with the concept of exception management in that it describes a policy where absolute focus is on exception management, in contrast to moderate application of exception management.

   a. Cash cow
   b. Best practice
   c. Management by exception
   d. Performance measurement

5. Government _____ are designed to show nonfinancial aspects of government operations. For example, a government financial report might include the number of arrests, number of convictions by crime category as well as the change (i.e., increase or decrease) in crime rate. Government _____ usually provide data on environmental conditions, education and conditions of streets and roads.
   a. BMC Software, Inc.
   b. 3M Company
   c. BNSF Railway
   d. Performance reports

6. Project _____: The project _____ is a prediction of the costs associated with a particular company project. These costs include labor, materials, and other related expenses. The project _____ is often broken down into specific tasks, with task _____s assigned to each.

Chapter 12. Responsibility Accounting, Quality Control, and Environmental Cost Management

a. BMC Software, Inc.
c. Budget

b. BNSF Railway
d. 3M Company

7. In business, _____, Overhead cost or _____ expense refers to an ongoing expense of operating a business. The term _____ is usually used to group expenses that are necessary to the continued functioning of the business, but do not directly generate profits.

_____ expenses are all costs on the income statement except for direct labor and direct materials.

a. Overhead
c. Intangible assets

b. ABC Television Network
d. AIG

8. In probability theory and statistics, the _____ of a random variable, probability distribution averaging the squared distance of its possible values from the expected value (mean.) Whereas the mean is a way to describe the location of a distribution, the _____ is a way to capture its scale or degree of being spread out. The unit of _____ is the square of the unit of the original variable.

a. Statistics
c. Monte Carlo methods

b. Time series
d. Variance

9. In statistics, _____ (ANOVA) is a collection of statistical models, and their associated procedures, in which the observed variance is partitioned into components due to different explanatory variables. In its simplest form ANOVA gives a statistical test of whether the means of several groups are all equal, and therefore generalizes Student's two-sample t-test to more than two groups.

There are three conceptual classes of such models:

1. Fixed-effects models assumes that the data came from normal populations which may differ only in their means. (Model 1)
2. Random effects models assume that the data describe a hierarchy of different populations whose differences are constrained by the hierarchy. (Model 2)
3. Mixed-effect models describe situations where both fixed and random effects are present. (Model 3)

In practice, there are several types of ANOVA depending on the number of treatments and the way they are applied to the subjects in the experiment:

- One-way ANOVA is used to test for differences among two or more independent groups. Typically, however, the one-way ANOVA is used to test for differences among at least three groups, since the two-group case can be covered by a T-test (Gossett, 1908.)

a. IMF
c. Open database connectivity

b. Analysis of variance
d. Intergenerational equity

10. A _____ is a tangible input for a product manufactured/Service provided, like labor or material. For example a cloth manufacturing firm requires some amount of predetermined labor and predetermined raw material for any amount of cloth being manufactured. The cost of employing labor can be directly fixed as 'per man per hour' or 'per man per day', so the labor is a _____ as you can directly associate cost with it.

Chapter 12. Responsibility Accounting, Quality Control, and Environmental Cost Management

a. Round-tripping
c. Residual value
b. 3M Company
d. Cost object

11. _____ is a costing model that identifies activities in an organization and assigns the cost of each activity resource to all products and services according to the actual consumption by each: it assigns more indirect costs (overhead) into direct costs.

In this way an organization can establish the true cost of its individual products and services for the purposes of identifying and eliminating those which are unprofitable and lowering the prices of those which are overpriced.

In a business organization, the ABC methodology assigns an organization's resource costs through activities to the products and services provided to its customers.

a. Indirect costs
c. ABC Television Network
b. Activity-based costing
d. Activity-based management

12. _____ is an important property of a control system, and the _____ property plays a crucial role in many control problems, such as stabilization of unstable systems by feedback, or optimal control.

_____ and observability are dual aspects of the same problem.

Roughly, the concept of _____ denotes the ability to move a system around in its entire configuration space using only certain admissible manipulations.

a. Controllable
c. BMC Software, Inc.
b. 3M Company
d. Controllability

13. In economics and sociology, an _____ is any factor (financial or non-financial) that enables or motivates a particular course of action, or counts as a reason for preferring one choice to the alternatives. It is an expectation that encourages people to behave in a certain way. Since human beings are purposeful creatures, the study of _____ structures is central to the study of all economic activity (both in terms of individual decision-making and in terms of co-operation and competition within a larger institutional structure.)

a. ABC Television Network
c. AIG
b. AMEX
d. Incentive

14. In mathematics _____s are numbers or other things that get multiplied. In particular, see:

- Factorization, the decomposition of an object into a product of other objects
- Integer factorization, the process of breaking down a composite number into smaller non-trivial divisors
- A coefficient
- A divisor of a particular number, or of an element of a monoid
- A von Neumann algebra with a trivial center

Chapter 12. Responsibility Accounting, Quality Control, and Environmental Cost Management 77

In statistics

- _____ analysis is the study of how _____s or certain variables affect variables.

In technology:

- Human _____s, a profession that focuses on how people interact with products, tools, or procedures
- 'Functionality, Application domain, Conditions, Technology, Objects and Responsibility;', In object-oriented programming

In computer science and information technology:

- Authentication _____, a piece of information used to verify a person's identity for security purposes
- _____, a Unix command for numbers factorization
- _____ (programming language), an experimental Forth-like programming language

In television:

- The O'Reilly _____, an American talk show hosted by Bill O'Reilly on Fox News.
- The Krypton _____, a British game show hosted by Gordon Burns, formally on ITV. Also had an American version.

.

   a. Merck ' Co., Inc.   b. The Goodyear Tire ' Rubber Company
   c. Valuation   d. Factor

15. _____ is a company's financial statement that indicates how the revenue is transformed into the net income The purpose of the _____ is to show managers and investors whether the company made or lost money during the period being reported.

The important thing to remember about an _____ is that it represents a period of time.

   a. Income statement   b. ABC Television Network
   c. AMEX   d. AIG

16. _____, in managerial economics is a form of cost accounting. It is a simplified model, useful for elementary instruction and for short-run decisions.

Cost-volume-profit (CVP) analysis expands the use of information provided by breakeven analysis.

   a. Cost accounting   b. Cost of quality
   c. Fixed costs   d. Cost-volume-profit analysis

Chapter 12. Responsibility Accounting, Quality Control, and Environmental Cost Management

17. The International Organization for Standardization (Organisation internationale de normalisation), widely known as _____ , is an international-standard-setting body composed of representatives from various national standards organizations. Founded on 23 February 1947, the organization promulgates worldwide proprietary industrial and commercial standards. It is headquartered in Geneva, Switzerland.

   a. ISO
   b. ABC Television Network
   c. AIG
   d. AMEX

18. _____ is a business management strategy aimed at embedding awareness of quality in all organizational processes. _____ has been widely used in manufacturing, education, call centers, government, and service industries, as well as NASA space and science programs.

When used together as a phrase, the three words in this expression have the following meanings:

- Total: Involving the entire organization, supply chain, and/or product life cycle
- Quality: With its usual definitions, with all its complexities
- Management: The system of managing with steps like Plan, Organize, Control, Lead, Staff, provisioning and organizing.

As defined by the International Organization for Standardization (ISO):

'_____ is a management approach for an organization, centered on quality, based on the participation of all its members and aiming at long-term success through customer satisfaction, and benefits to all members of the organization and to society.' ISO 8402:1994

One major aim is to reduce variation from every process so that greater consistency of effort is obtained. (Royse, D., Thyer, B., Padgett D., ' Logan T., 2006)

In Japan, _____ comprises four process steps, namely:

1. Kaizen - Focuses on 'Continuous Process Improvement', to make processes visible, repeatable and measurable.
2. Atarimae Hinshitsu - The idea that 'things will work as they are supposed to' .
3. Kansei - Examining the way the user applies the product leads to improvement in the product itself.
4. Miryokuteki Hinshitsu - The idea that 'things should have an aesthetic quality' (for example, a pen will write in a way that is pleasing to the writer.)

_____ requires that the company maintain this quality standard in all aspects of its business. This requires ensuring that things are done right the first time and that defects and waste are eliminated from operations.

   a. BMC Software, Inc.
   b. BNSF Railway
   c. Total quality management
   d. 3M Company

Chapter 12. Responsibility Accounting, Quality Control, and Environmental Cost Management

19. An _____ is a term used in behavioral economics to describe those types of behaviors that impose costs on a person in the long-run that are not taken into account when making decisions in the present. Classical Economics discourages government from creating legislation that targets internalities, because it is assumed that the consumer takes these personal costs into account when paying for the good that causes the _____. For example, cigarettes should be taxed because of the negative consumption externalities that they impose, such as second-hand smoke, not because the smoker harms him or herself by smoking.

   a. Authorised capital
   b. Operating budget
   c. Inventory turnover ratio
   d. Internality

20. _____ can be defined as the idea generation, concept development, testing and manufacturing or implementation of a physical object or service. _____ers conceptualize and evaluate ideas, making them tangible through products in a more systematic approach. The role of a _____er encompasses many characteristics of the marketing manager, product manager, industrial designer and design engineer.

   a. Alan Greenspan
   b. Arthur Betz Laffer
   c. Abby Joseph Cohen
   d. Product design

21. The concept of _____ is a means to quantify the total cost of quality-related efforts and deficiencies. It was first described by Armand V. Feigenbaum in a 1956 Harvard Business Review article.

Prior to its introduction, the general perception was that higher quality requires higher costs, either by buying better materials or machines or by hiring more labor.

   a. Quality costs
   b. Cost allocation
   c. Variable cost
   d. Marginal cost

22. _____ is a business management strategy, initially implemented by Motorola, that today enjoys widespread application in many sectors of industry.

_____ seeks to improve the quality of process outputs by identifying and removing the causes of defects (errors) and variation in manufacturing and business processes. It uses a set of quality management methods, including statistical methods, and creates a special infrastructure of people within the organization ('Black Belts' etc.)

   a. Theory of constraints
   b. Six Sigma
   c. Lean manufacturing
   d. Make to order

23. '_____' is Step 7 of 'Philip Crosby's 14 Step Quality Improvement Process'. Although applicable to any type of enterprise, it has been primarily adopted within industry supply chains wherever large volumes of components are being purchased (common items such as nuts and bolts are good examples.)

_____ was a quality control program originated by the Denver Division of the Martin Marietta Corporation (now Lockheed Martin) on the Titan Missile program, which carried the first astronauts into space in the late 1960s.

a. 3M Company
b. BMC Software, Inc.
c. BNSF Railway
d. Zero defects

24. _____ is a family of standards for quality management systems. _____ is maintained by ISO, the International Organization for Standardization and is administered by accreditation and certification bodies. The rules are updated, the time and changes in the requirements for quality, motivate change.

a. AMEX
b. AIG
c. ABC Television Network
d. ISO 9000

25. _____ is a pattern of resource use that aims to meet human needs while preserving the environment so that these needs can be met not only in the present, but also for future generations to come. The term was used by the Brundtland Commission which coined what has become the most often-quoted definition of _____ as development that 'meets the needs of the present without compromising the ability of future generations to meet their own needs.'

_____ ties together concern for the carrying capacity of natural systems with the social challenges facing humanity. As early as the 1970s 'sustainability' was employed to describe an economy 'in equilibrium with basic ecological support systems.' Ecologists have pointed to the e;limits of growthe; and presented the alternative of a e;steady state economye; in order to address environmental concerns.

a. Collusion
b. Limited liability company
c. Sustainable development
d. Time value of money

26. _____ is the process whereby companies use cost accounting to report or control the various costs of doing business.

The term _____ is widely used in business today. Unfortunately _____ has no uniform definition.

a. Contribution margin
b. Process costing
c. Cost management
d. Contribution margin analysis

Chapter 13. Investment Centers and Transfer Pricing

1. An _____ is a classification used for business units within an enterprise. The essential element of an _____ is that it is treated as a unit which is measured against its use of capital, as opposed to a cost or profit center, which are measured against raw costs or profits.

The advantage of this form of measurement is that it tends to be more encompassing, since it accounts for all uses of capital.

   a. ABC Television Network
   b. AIG
   c. Investment center
   d. AMEX

2. _____ is a process of agreeing upon objectives within an organization so that management and employees agree to the objectives and understand what they are in the organization.

The term '_____' was first popularized by Peter Drucker in his 1954 book 'The Practice of Management'.

The essence of _____ is participative goal setting, choosing course of actions and decision making.

   a. Cash cow
   b. Best practice
   c. Trustee
   d. Management by objectives

3. _____ is one of the four Ps of the marketing mix. The other three aspects are product, promotion, and place. It is also a key variable in microeconomic price allocation theory.

   a. Target costing
   b. Pricing
   c. Cost-plus pricing
   d. Price

4. _____ can be regarded as an outcome of mental processes (cognitive process) leading to the selection of a course of action among several alternatives. Every _____ process produces a final choice. The output can be an action or an opinion of choice.

   a. Decision making
   b. BNSF Railway
   c. BMC Software, Inc.
   d. 3M Company

5. _____ in economics and business is the result of an exchange and from that trade we assign a numerical monetary value to a good, service or asset. If Alice trades Bob 4 apples for an orange, the _____ of an orange is 4 apples. Inversely, the _____ of an apple is 1/4 oranges.

   a. Transactional Net Margin Method
   b. Price discrimination
   c. Discounts and allowances
   d. Price

6. _____ is the process whereby an organization establishes the parameters within which programs, investments, and acquisitions are reaching the desired results. Performance Reference Model of the Federal Enterprise Architecture, 2005.

This process of measuring performance often requires the use of statistical evidence to determine progress toward specific defined organizational objectives.

There are many types of measurements.

a. Management by exception
b. Performance measurement
c. Trustee
d. Management by objectives

7. In economics, _____ or _____ goods or real _____ refers to factors of production used to create goods or services that are not themselves significantly consumed (though they may depreciate) in the production process. _____ goods may be acquired with money or financial _____. In finance and accounting, _____ generally refers to financial wealth, especially that used to start or maintain a business.

a. Screening
b. Capital
c. Vyborg Appeal
d. Disclosure

8. _____ is systematic determination of merit, worth, and significance of something or someone using criteria against a set of standards. _____ often is used to characterize and appraise subjects of interest in a wide range of human enterprises, including the arts, criminal justice, foundations and non-profit organizations, government, health care, and other human services.

Depending on the topic of interest, there are professional groups which look to the quality and rigor of the _____ process.

a. AIG
b. AMEX
c. ABC Television Network
d. Evaluation

9. _____ represents the total cash investment that shareholders and debtholders have made in a company. There are two different but completely equivalent methods for calculating _____. The operating approach is calculated as:

_____ = Operating Net Working Capital + Net PP'E + Capitalized Operating Leases + Other Operating Assets + Operating Intangibles - Other Operating Liabilities - Cumulative Adjustment for Amortization of R'D

Equivalently, the financing approach is calculated as:

In symbols:

$$K = D + E - M$$

_____ is used in several important measurements of financial performance, including return on _____, economic value added, and free cash flow.

a. AlphaIC
b. Equity ratio
c. Average propensity to consume
d. Invested capital

10. In finance, _____ also known as return on investment, rate of profit or sometimes just return, is the ratio of money gained or lost on an investment relative to the amount of money invested. The amount of money gained or lost may be referred to as interest, profit/loss, gain/loss, or net income/loss. The money invested may be referred to as the asset, capital, principal, or the cost basis of the investment.

Chapter 13. Investment Centers and Transfer Pricing

a. Rate of return
c. Capital employed
b. Theoretical ex-rights price
d. Debt to capital ratio

11. In mathematics _____s are numbers or other things that get multiplied. In particular, see:

- Factorization, the decomposition of an object into a product of other objects
- Integer factorization, the process of breaking down a composite number into smaller non-trivial divisors
- A coefficient
- A divisor of a particular number, or of an element of a monoid
- A von Neumann algebra with a trivial center

In statistics

- _____ analysis is the study of how _____s or certain variables affect variables.

In technology:

- Human _____s, a profession that focuses on how people interact with products, tools, or procedures
- 'Functionality, Application domain, Conditions, Technology, Objects and Responsibility;', In object-oriented programming

In computer science and information technology:

- Authentication _____, a piece of information used to verify a person's identity for security purposes
- _____, a Unix command for numbers factorization
- _____ (programming language), an experimental Forth-like programming language

In television:

- The O'Reilly _____, an American talk show hosted by Bill O'Reilly on Fox News.
- The Krypton _____, a British game show hosted by Gordon Burns, formally on ITV. Also had an American version.

a. Valuation
c. Merck ' Co., Inc.
b. The Goodyear Tire ' Rubber Company
d. Factor

12. A _____ is the pinnacle activity involved in selling products or services in return for money or other compensation. It is an act of completion of a commercial activity.

A _____ is completed by the seller, the owner of the goods.

a. Tertiary sector of economy
c. High yield stock
b. Sale
d. Maturity

Chapter 13. Investment Centers and Transfer Pricing

13. In corporate finance, _____ or _____ is an estimate of true economic profit after making corrective adjustments to GAAP accounting, including deducting the opportunity cost of equity capital. _____ can be measured as Net Operating Profit After Taxes(or NOPAT) less the money cost of capital. _____ is similar in nature to that of calculating another financial performance measure - Residual Income , however, there are a few complexities involved with coming up with the elements for calculating _____ over RI such as the myriad adjustments that might be made to NOPAT before it is suitable for the formula below.

   a. Outsourcing
   b. International Monetary Fund
   c. Internal control
   d. Economic value added

14. A mutual shareholder or _____ is an individual or company (including a corporation) that legally owns one or more shares of stock in a joint stock company. A company's shareholders collectively own that company. Thus, the typical goal of such companies is to enhance shareholder value.

   a. Growth investing
   b. 3M Company
   c. Stock split
   d. Stockholder

15. _____ refers to the additional value of a commodity over the cost of commodities used to produce it from the previous stage of production. An example is the price of gasoline at the pump over the price of the oil in it. In national accounts used in macroeconomics, it refers to the contribution of the factors of production, i.e., land, labor, and capital goods, to raising the value of a product and corresponds to the incomes received by the owners of these factors.

   a. Minimum wage
   b. Supply-side economics
   c. 3M Company
   d. Value added

16. In economics, business, retail, and accounting, a _____ is the value of money that has been used up to produce something, and hence is not available for use anymore. In economics, a _____ is an alternative that is given up as a result of a decision. In business, the _____ may be one of acquisition, in which case the amount of money expended to acquire it is counted as _____.

   a. Prime cost
   b. Cost
   c. Cost allocation
   d. Cost of quality

17. The _____ is an expected return that the provider of capital plans to earn on their investment.

Capital (money) used for funding a business should earn returns for the capital providers who risk their capital. For an investment to be worthwhile, the expected return on capital must be greater than the _____.

   a. 3M Company
   b. BMC Software, Inc.
   c. Capital flight
   d. Cost of capital

18. In economics and sociology, an _____ is any factor (financial or non-financial) that enables or motivates a particular course of action, or counts as a reason for preferring one choice to the alternatives. It is an expectation that encourages people to behave in a certain way. Since human beings are purposeful creatures, the study of _____ structures is central to the study of all economic activity (both in terms of individual decision-making and in terms of co-operation and competition within a larger institutional structure.)

   a. Incentive
   b. AIG
   c. AMEX
   d. ABC Television Network

Chapter 13. Investment Centers and Transfer Pricing

19. _____ is a term describing performance-related pay, most frequently in the context of educational reform. It provides bonuses for workers who perform their jobs better, according to measurable criteria. In the United States, policy makers are divided on whether _____ should be offered to public school teachers, as is commonly the case in the United Kingdom.
   a. Retirement plan
   b. 3M Company
   c. BMC Software, Inc.
   d. Merit pay

20. In accounting, _____ or carrying value is the value of an asset according to its balance sheet account balance. For assets, the value is based on the original cost of the asset less any depreciation, amortization or impairment costs made against the asset. Traditionally, a company's _____ is its total assets minus intangible assets and liabilities.
   a. Depreciation
   b. Book value
   c. Generally accepted accounting principles
   d. Matching principle

21. In accounting, _____ is the original monetary value of an economic item. In some circumstances, assets and liabilities may be shown at their _____, as if there had been no change in value since the date of acquisition. The balance sheet value of the item may therefore differ from the 'true' value.
   a. Matching principle
   b. Cost of goods sold
   c. Bottom line
   d. Historical cost

22. An _____ is the buying of one company by another. An _____ may be friendly or hostile. In the former case, the companies cooperate in negotiations; in the latter case, the takeover target is unwilling to be bought or the target's board has no prior knowledge of the offer. _____ usually refers to a purchase of a smaller firm by a larger one. Sometimes, however, a smaller firm will acquire management control of a larger or longer established company and keep its name for the combined entity. This is known as a reverse takeover.
   a. AIG
   b. AMEX
   c. ABC Television Network
   d. Acquisition

23. In business and accounting, _____ are everything of value that is owned by a person or company. It is a claim on the property your income of a borrower. The balance sheet of a firm records the monetary value of the _____ owned by the firm.
   a. Accrual basis accounting
   b. Accounts receivable
   c. Earnings before interest, taxes, depreciation and amortization
   d. Assets

24. In accounting, _____ are considered liabilities of the business that are to be settled in cash within the fiscal year or the operating cycle, whichever period is longer.

For example accounts payable for goods, services or supplies that were purchased for use in the operation of the business and payable within a normal period of time would be _____.

Bonds, mortgages and loans that are payable over a term exceeding one year would be fixed liabilities.

   a. Payroll
   b. Treasury stock
   c. Closing entries
   d. Current liabilities

Chapter 13. Investment Centers and Transfer Pricing

25. In financial accounting, a _____ is defined as an obligation of an entity arising from past transactions or events, the settlement of which may result in the transfer or use of assets, provision of services or other yielding of economic benefits in the future.

   a. Vested
   b. Liability
   c. False Claims Act
   d. Corporate governance

26. _____ is the strategy an investor uses to distribute his or her investments among various classes of investment vehicles (e.g., stocks and bonds.)

A large part of financial planning is finding an _____ that is appropriate for a given person in terms of their appetite for and ability to shoulder risk. This can depend on various factors; see investor profile.

   a. ABC Television Network
   b. Incremental capital-output ratio
   c. AIG
   d. Asset allocation

27. The term _____ has three unrelated technical definitions, and is also used in a variety of non-technical ways.

- In financial economics, it refers to any asset used to make money, as opposed to assets used for personal enjoyment or consumption. This is an important distinction because two people can disagree sharply about the value of personal assets, one person might think a sports car is more valuable than a pickup truck, another person might have the opposite taste. But if an asset is held for the purpose of making money, taste has nothing to do with it, only differences of opinion about how much money the asset will produce. With the further assumption that people agree on the probability distribution of future cash flows, it is possible to have an objective _____ pricing model. Even without the assumption of agreement, it is possible to set rational limits on _____ value.
- In governmental accounting, it is defined as any asset used in operations with an initial useful life extending beyond one reporting period. Generally, government managers have a 'stewardship' duty to maintain _____ s under their control. See International Public Sector Accounting Standards for details.
- In US tax accounting, it is defined as any property other than a list of exceptions. The main exceptions are anything held for sale, and any real estate or depreciable property used in business. Almost everything you own and use for personal purposes, pleasure or investment is a _____. If something is a _____ for tax purposes, gains or losses on sale or disposition are capital gains or capital losses. For individuals, however, capital losses on property held for personal use are generally not deductible. See the IRS publication Tax Facts about Capital Gains and Losses for details.

A well-known financial accounting textbook advises that the term be avoided except in tax accounting because it is used in so many different senses, not all of them well-defined. For example it is often used as a synonym for fixed assets or for investments in securities.

A common non-technical usage occurs when people ask that employees or the environment or something else be treated as a _____.

   a. Capital asset
   b. BMC Software, Inc.
   c. Solvency
   d. 3M Company

28. In economics, _____ is a rise in the general level of prices of goods and services in an economy over a period of time. When the general price level rises, each unit of currency buys fewer goods and services; consequently, _____ is also a decline in the real value of money--a loss of purchasing power in the medium of exchange which is also the monetary unit of account in the economy. A chief measure of general price-level _____ is the general _____ rate, which is the percentage change in a general price index (normally the Consumer Price Index) over time.

    a. ABC Television Network
    b. Opportunity cost
    c. AIG
    d. Inflation

29. _____ is an area of engineering practice concerned with the 'application of scientific principles and techniques to problems of cost estimating, cost control, business planning and management science, profitability analysis, project management, and planning and scheduling.'

Key objectives of _____ are to arrive at accurate cost estimates and to avoid cost overruns. The broad array of _____ topics represent the intersection of the fields of project management, business management, and engineering. Most people have a limited view of what engineering encompasses.

    a. BNSF Railway
    b. BMC Software, Inc.
    c. Cost engineering
    d. 3M Company

30. _____ is the calculated approximation of a result which is usable even if input data may be incomplete or uncertain.

In statistics, see _____ theory, estimator.

In mathematics, approximation or _____ typically means finding upper or lower bounds of a quantity that cannot readily be computed precisely and is also an educated guess .

    a. AIG
    b. Estimation
    c. ABC Television Network
    d. AMEX

31. The _____ is a performance management tool which began as a concept for measuring whether the smaller-scale operational activities of a company are aligned with its larger-scale objectives in terms of vision and strategy.

By focusing not only on financial outcomes but also on the operational, marketing and developmental inputs to these, the _____ helps provide a more comprehensive view of a business, which in turn helps organizations act in their best long-term interests. This tool is also being used to address business response to climate change and greenhouse gas emissions.

    a. Trustee
    b. Management by objectives
    c. Best practice
    d. Balanced scorecard

32. _____ is concerned with the provisions and use of accounting information to managers within organizations, to provide them with the basis to make informed business decisions that will allow them to be better equipped in their management and control functions.

In contrast to financial accountancy information, _____ information is:

- usually confidential and used by management, instead of publicly reported;
- forward-looking, instead of historical;
- pragmatically computed using extensive management information systems and internal controls, instead of complying with accounting standards.

This is because of the different emphasis: _____ information is used within an organization, typically for decision-making.

    a. Nonassurance services   b. Governmental accounting
    c. Grenzplankostenrechnung   d. Management accounting

33. A _____ is any one of a variety of different systems, institutions, procedures, social relations and infrastructures whereby persons trade, and goods and services are exchanged, forming part of the economy. It is an arrangement that allows buyers and sellers to exchange things. _____s vary in size, range, geographic scale, location, types and variety of human communities, as well as the types of goods and services traded.
    a. Market   b. Perfect competition
    c. Recession   d. Market Failure

34. _____ is an economic concept with commonplace familiarity. It is the price that a good or service is offered at, or will fetch, in the marketplace. It is of interest mainly in the study of microeconomics.
    a. Spot rate   b. Financial instruments
    c. Market price   d. Transfer agent

35. _____ or economic opportunity loss is the value of the next best alternative foregone as the result of making a decision. _____ analysis is an important part of a company's decision-making processes but is not treated as an actual cost in any financial statement. The next best thing that a person can engage in is referred to as the _____ of doing the best thing and ignoring the next best thing to be done.
    a. ABC Television Network   b. Inflation
    c. AIG   d. Opportunity cost

36. Total _____ is a method of Accounting cost which entails the full cost of manufacturing or providing a service. This includes not just the costs of materials and labour, but also of all manufacturing overheads (whether e;fixede; or e;variablee;.) One of the main reasons for absorbing overheads into the cost of units is for inventory valuation purposes.
    a. ABC Television Network   b. AIG
    c. AMEX   d. Absorption costing

37. _____ is the process of comparing the cost, cycle time, productivity, or quality of a specific process or method to another that is widely considered to be an industry standard or best practice. Essentially, _____ provides a snapshot of the performance of your business and helps you understand where you are in relation to a particular standard. The result is often a business case for making changes in order to make improvements.
    a. 3M Company   b. Benchmarking
    c. BMC Software, Inc.   d. Strategic business unit

Chapter 13. Investment Centers and Transfer Pricing

38. _____ is a concept in economics which refers to the extent to which an enterprise or a nation actually uses its installed productive capacity. Thus, it refers to the relationship between actual output that 'is' produced with the installed equipment and the potential output which 'could' be produced with it, if capacity was fully used.

If market demand grows, _____ will rise.

   a. Long-run
   c. BMC Software, Inc.
   b. 3M Company
   d. Capacity utilization

39. In economic theory, _____ is the competitive situation in any market where the conditions necessary for perfect competition are not satisfied. It is a market structure that does not meet the conditions of perfect competition.

Forms of _____ include:

- Monopoly, in which there is only one seller of a good.
- Oligopoly, in which there is a small number of sellers.
- Monopolistic competition, in which there are many sellers producing highly differentiated goods.
- Monopsony, in which there is only one buyer of a good.
- Oligopsony, in which there is a small number of buyers.

There may also be _____ in markets due to buyers or sellers lacking information about prices and the goods being traded.

There may also be _____ due to a time lag in a market.

   a. AMEX
   c. Imperfect competition
   b. ABC Television Network
   d. AIG

40. In neoclassical economics and microeconomics, _____ describes the perfect being a market in which there are many small firms, all producing homogeneous goods. In the short term, such markets are productively inefficient as output will not occur where mc is equal to ac, but allocatively efficient, as output under _____ will always occur where mc is equal to mr, and therefore where mc equals ar. However, in the long term, such markets are both allocatively and productively efficient.

   a. Market Failure
   c. Nominal value
   b. Market
   d. Perfect competition

41. _____ accounting (Full costA) generally refers to the process of collecting and presenting information (costs as well as advantages) for each proposed alternative when a decision is necessary. A synonym, true cost accounting (TCA) is also often used. Experts consider both terms problematic as definitions of 'true' and 'full' are inherently subjective

   a. 3M Company
   c. BNSF Railway
   b. Full cost
   d. BMC Software, Inc.

42. An _____ is a tax levied on the financial income of people, corporations, or other legal entities. Various _____ systems exist, with varying degrees of tax incidence. Income taxation can be progressive, proportional, or regressive.

Chapter 13. Investment Centers and Transfer Pricing

    a. Ordinary income
    b. Individual Retirement Arrangement
    c. Income tax
    d. Implied level of government service

43. In physics, and more specifically kinematics, _____ is the change in velocity over time. Because velocity is a vector, it can change in two ways: a change in magnitude and/or a change in direction. In one dimension, _____ is the rate at which something speeds up or slows down.
    a. ABC Television Network
    b. AIG
    c. AMEX
    d. Acceleration

44. _____ refers to any one of several methods by which a company, for 'financial accounting' and/or tax purposes, depreciates a fixed asset in such a way that the amount of depreciation taken each year is higher during the earlier years of an assete;s life. For financial accounting purposes, _____ is generally used when an asset is expected to be much more productive during its early years, so that depreciation expense will more accurately represent how much of an assete;s usefulness is being used up each year. For tax purposes, _____ provides a way of deferring corporate income taxes by reducing taxable income in current years, in exchange for increased taxable income in future years.
    a. Effective marginal tax rates
    b. User charge
    c. Indirect tax
    d. Accelerated depreciation

45. _____ is a term used in accounting, economics and finance to spread the cost of an asset over the span of several years.

In simple words we can say that _____ is the reduction in the value of an asset due to usage, passage of time, wear and tear, technological outdating or obsolescence, depletion, inadequacy, rot, rust, decay or other such factors.

In accounting, _____ is a term used to describe any method of attributing the historical or purchase cost of an asset across its useful life, roughly corresponding to normal wear and tear.

    a. Current asset
    b. Depreciation
    c. General ledger
    d. Net profit

46. An _____ is a term used in behavioral economics to describe those types of behaviors that impose costs on a person in the long-run that are not taken into account when making decisions in the present. Classical Economics discourages government from creating legislation that targets internalities, because it is assumed that the consumer takes these personal costs into account when paying for the good that causes the _____. For example, cigarettes should be taxed because of the negative consumption externalities that they impose, such as second-hand smoke, not because the smoker harms him or herself by smoking.
    a. Inventory turnover ratio
    b. Operating budget
    c. Internality
    d. Authorised capital

47. In accounting and organizational theory, _____ is defined as a process effected by an organization's structure, work and authority flows, people and management information systems, designed to help the organization accomplish specific goals or objectives. It is a means by which an organization's resources are directed, monitored, and measured. It plays an important role in preventing and detecting fraud and protecting the organization's resources, both physical (e.g., machinery and property) and intangible (e.g., reputation or intellectual property such as trademarks.)

a. Audit committee
c. Auditor independence
b. Audit risk
d. Internal control

48. _____ is a concept that denotes the precise probability of specific eventualities. Technically, the notion of _____ is independent from the notion of value and, as such, eventualities may have both beneficial and adverse consequences. However, in general usage the convention is to focus only on potential negative impact to some characteristic of value that may arise from a future event.

   a. Discount factor
   c. Discounting
   b. Risk
   d. Risk adjusted return on capital

49. _____ is a concept in economics, finance, and psychology related to the behaviour of consumers and investors under uncertainty. _____ is the reluctance of a person to accept a bargain with an uncertain payoff rather than another bargain with a more certain, but possibly lower, expected payoff. For example, a risk-averse investor might choose to put his or her money into a bank account with a low but guaranteed interest rate, rather than into a stock that is likely to have high returns, but also has a chance of becoming worthless.

   a. Risk adjusted return on capital
   c. Discount factor
   b. Risk
   d. Risk aversion

50. _____ is a costing model that identifies activities in an organization and assigns the cost of each activity resource to all products and services according to the actual consumption by each: it assigns more indirect costs (overhead) into direct costs.

In this way an organization can establish the true cost of its individual products and services for the purposes of identifying and eliminating those which are unprofitable and lowering the prices of those which are overpriced.

In a business organization, the ABC methodology assigns an organization's resource costs through activities to the products and services provided to its customers.

   a. ABC Television Network
   c. Indirect costs
   b. Activity-based costing
   d. Activity-based management

51. The _____ is one of the three economic sectors, the others being the secondary sector (approximately manufacturing) and the primary sector (extraction such as mining, agriculture and fishing.) Sometimes an additional sector, the 'quaternary sector', is defined for the sharing of information (which normally belongs to the tertiary sector.)

The tertiary sector is defined by exclusion of the two other sectors.

   a. Tertiary sector of economy
   c. Capital
   b. Just-in-time
   d. Low Income Housing Tax Credit

52. _____, a form of pecuniary corruption, is an act implying money or gift given that alters the behaviour of the recipient. _____ constitutes a crime and is defined by Black's Law Dictionary as the offering, giving, receiving, or soliciting of any item of value to influence the actions of an official or other person in discharge of a public or legal duty. The bribe is the gift bestowed to influence the recipient's conduct.

a. BNSF Railway
b. BMC Software, Inc.
c. Bribery
d. 3M Company

53. The _____ of 1977 (15 U.S.C. §§ 78dd-1, et seq.) is a United States federal law known primarily for two of its main provisions, one that addresses accounting transparency requirements under the Securities Exchange Act of 1934 and another concerning bribery of foreign officials.
  a. Pre-emption right
  b. Lease
  c. Competition law
  d. Foreign Corrupt Practices Act

54. Internal auditing is a profession and activity involved in helping organisations achieve their stated objectives. It does this by utilizing a systematic methodology for analyzing business processes, procedures and activities with the goal of highlighting organizational problems and recommending solutions. Professionals called _____ are employed by organizations to perform the internal auditing activity.
  a. Auditor independence
  b. Internal auditors
  c. Internal Auditing
  d. Auditing Standards Board

Chapter 14. Decision Making; Relevant Costs and Benefits

1. _____ is concerned with the provisions and use of accounting information to managers within organizations, to provide them with the basis to make informed business decisions that will allow them to be better equipped in their management and control functions.

In contrast to financial accountancy information, _____ information is:

- usually confidential and used by management, instead of publicly reported;
- forward-looking, instead of historical;
- pragmatically computed using extensive management information systems and internal controls, instead of complying with accounting standards.

This is because of the different emphasis: _____ information is used within an organization, typically for decision-making.

a. Management accounting
c. Governmental accounting
b. Grenzplankostenrechnung
d. Nonassurance services

2. _____ is one of the four Ps of the marketing mix. The other three aspects are product, promotion, and place. It is also a key variable in microeconomic price allocation theory.
a. Price
c. Target costing
b. Cost-plus pricing
d. Pricing

3. In economics, business, retail, and accounting, a _____ is the value of money that has been used up to produce something, and hence is not available for use anymore. In economics, a _____ is an alternative that is given up as a result of a decision. In business, the _____ may be one of acquisition, in which case the amount of money expended to acquire it is counted as _____.
a. Prime cost
c. Cost of quality
b. Cost allocation
d. Cost

4. _____ is a costing model that identifies activities in an organization and assigns the cost of each activity resource to all products and services according to the actual consumption by each: it assigns more indirect costs (overhead) into direct costs.

In this way an organization can establish the true cost of its individual products and services for the purposes of identifying and eliminating those which are unprofitable and lowering the prices of those which are overpriced.

In a business organization, the ABC methodology assigns an organization's resource costs through activities to the products and services provided to its customers.

a. Indirect costs
c. Activity-based costing
b. Activity-based management
d. ABC Television Network

5. In accounting, _____ or carrying value is the value of an asset according to its balance sheet account balance. For assets, the value is based on the original cost of the asset less any depreciation, amortization or impairment costs made against the asset. Traditionally, a company's _____ is its total assets minus intangible assets and liabilities.

Chapter 14. Decision Making; Relevant Costs and Benefits

    a. Depreciation
    b. Book value
    c. Generally accepted accounting principles
    d. Matching principle

6. _____ is a term used in accounting, economics and finance to spread the cost of an asset over the span of several years.

In simple words we can say that _____ is the reduction in the value of an asset due to usage, passage of time, wear and tear, technological outdating or obsolescence, depletion, inadequacy, rot, rust, decay or other such factors.

In accounting, _____ is a term used to describe any method of attributing the historical or purchase cost of an asset across its useful life, roughly corresponding to normal wear and tear.

    a. General ledger
    b. Net profit
    c. Current asset
    d. Depreciation

7. In accounting, _____ is the original monetary value of an economic item. In some circumstances, assets and liabilities may be shown at their _____, as if there had been no change in value since the date of acquisition. The balance sheet value of the item may therefore differ from the 'true' value.

    a. Cost of goods sold
    b. Historical cost
    c. Bottom line
    d. Matching principle

8. _____ refers to an excess amount of information being provided, making processing and absorbing tasks very difficult for the individual because sometimes we cannot see the validity behind the information. As the world moves into a new era of globalization, an increasing number of people are logging onto the internet to conduct their own research and are given the ability to produce as well as consume the data accessed on an increasing number of websites. As of February 2007 there were over 108 million distinct websites and increasing.

    a. AMEX
    b. Information overload
    c. ABC Television Network
    d. AIG

9. In economics and business decision-making, _____ are costs that cannot be recovered once they have been incurred. _____ are sometimes contrasted with variable costs, which are the costs that will change due to the proposed course of action, and prospective costs which are costs that will be incurred if an action is taken.

In traditional microeconomic theory, only variable costs are relevant to a decision.

    a. BNSF Railway
    b. BMC Software, Inc.
    c. Sunk costs
    d. 3M Company

10. In physics, and more specifically kinematics, _____ is the change in velocity over time. Because velocity is a vector, it can change in two ways: a change in magnitude and/or a change in direction. In one dimension, _____ is the rate at which something speeds up or slows down.

    a. AIG
    b. Acceleration
    c. ABC Television Network
    d. AMEX

Chapter 14. Decision Making; Relevant Costs and Benefits

11. Total _____ is a method of Accounting cost which entails the full cost of manufacturing or providing a service. This includes not just the costs of materials and labour, but also of all manufacturing overheads (whether e;fixede; or e;variablee;.) One of the main reasons for absorbing overheads into the cost of units is for inventory valuation purposes.
   a. AIG
   b. ABC Television Network
   c. AMEX
   d. Absorption costing

12. _____ or economic opportunity loss is the value of the next best alternative foregone as the result of making a decision. _____ analysis is an important part of a company's decision-making processes but is not treated as an actual cost in any financial statement. The next best thing that a person can engage in is referred to as the _____ of doing the best thing and ignoring the next best thing to be done.
   a. AIG
   b. Inflation
   c. ABC Television Network
   d. Opportunity cost

13. _____ is a concept in economics which refers to the extent to which an enterprise or a nation actually uses its installed productive capacity. Thus, it refers to the relationship between actual output that 'is' produced with the installed equipment and the potential output which 'could' be produced with it, if capacity was fully used.

   If market demand grows, _____ will rise.

   a. BMC Software, Inc.
   b. Long-run
   c. 3M Company
   d. Capacity utilization

14. An _____ is a business that provides computer-based services to customers over a network. Software offered using an _____ model is also sometimes called On-demand software or software as a service (SaaS.) The most limited sense of this business is that of providing access to a particular application program (such as customer relationship management) using a standard protocol such as HTTP.
   a. Application service provider
   b. AIG
   c. ABC Television Network
   d. AMEX

15. _____ is a company-wide computer software system used to manage and coordinate all the resources, information, and functions of a business from shared data stores.

   An _____ system has a service-oriented architecture with modular hardware and software units or 'services' that communicate on a local area network. The modular design allows a business to add or reconfigure modules (perhaps from different vendors) while preserving data integrity in one shared database that may be centralized or distributed.

   a. ABC Television Network
   b. AMEX
   c. Enterprise resource planning
   d. AIG

16. _____ is subcontracting a process, such as product design or manufacturing, to a third-party company. The decision to outsource is often made in the interest of lowering cost or making better use of time and energy costs, redirecting or conserving energy directed at the competencies of a particular business, or to make more efficient use of land, labor, capital, (information) technology and resources. _____ became part of the business lexicon during the 1980s.

Chapter 14. Decision Making; Relevant Costs and Benefits

a. Outsourcing
c. Economic Growth and Tax Relief Reconciliation Act of 2001
b. US Airways, Inc.
d. USA Today

17. In accounting, _____ has a very specific meaning. It is an outflow of cash or other valuable assets from a person or company to another person or company. This outflow of cash is generally one side of a trade for products or services that have equal or better current or future value to the buyer than to the seller.

a. AMEX
b. ABC Television Network
c. Expense
d. AIG

18. In cost-volume-profit analysis, a form of management accounting, _____ is the marginal profit per unit sale. It is a useful quantity in carrying out various calculations, and can be used as a measure of operating leverage.

The Total _____ is Total Revenue (TR, or Sales) minus Total Variable Cost (TVC):

Tcontribution margin = TR − TVC

The Unit _____ (C) is Unit Revenue (Price, P) minus Unit Variable Cost (V):

C = P − V

The _____ Ratio is the percentage of Contribution over Total Revenue, which can be calculated from the unit contribution over unit price or total contribution over Total Revenue:

$$\frac{C}{P} = \frac{P-V}{P} = \frac{\text{Unit Contribution Margin}}{\text{Price}} = \frac{\text{Total Contribution Margin}}{\text{Total Revenue}}$$

For instance, if the price is $10 and the unit variable cost is $2, then the unit _____ is $8, and the _____ ratio is $8/$10 = 80%.

a. Cost management
b. Factory overhead
c. Profit center
d. Contribution margin

19. _____ is used to assign the available resources in an economic way. It is part of resource management.

In strategic planning, is a plan for using available resources, for example human resources, especially in the near term, to achieve goals for the future.

a. BNSF Railway
b. 3M Company
c. Resource allocation
d. BMC Software, Inc.

20. In mathematics, _____ is a technique for optimization of a linear objective function, subject to linear equality and linear inequality constraints. Informally, _____ determines the way to achieve the best outcome (such as maximum profit or lowest cost) in a given mathematical model and given some list of requirements represented as linear equations.

More formally, given a polytope (for example, a polygon or a polyhedron), and a real-valued affine function

$$f(x_1, x_2, \ldots, x_n) = c_1 x_1 + c_2 x_2 + \cdots + c_n x_n + d$$

defined on this polytope, a _____ method will find a point in the polytope where this function has the smallest (or largest) value.

a. BMC Software, Inc.
b. BNSF Railway
c. 3M Company
d. Linear programming

21. In probability theory and statistics, the _____ (or expectation value or mean and for continuous random variables with a density function it is the probability density -weighted integral of the possible values.

The term '_____' can be misleading.

a. Expected value
b. AIG
c. ABC Television Network
d. AMEX

22. _____ is the amount of time someone works beyond normal working hours. Normal hours may be determined in several ways:

- by custom (what is considered healthy or reasonable by society),
- by practices of a given trade or profession,
- by legislation,
- by agreement between employers and workers or their representatives.

Most nations have _____ laws designed to dissuade or prevent employers from forcing their employees to work excessively long hours. These laws may take into account other considerations than the humanitarian, such as increasing the overall level of employment in the economy. One common approach to regulating _____ is to require employers to pay workers at a higher hourly rate for _____ work.

a. ABC Television Network
b. AMEX
c. Overtime
d. AIG

23. _____ is the process of learning a new skill or trade, often in response to a change in the economic environment. Generally it reflects changes in profession choice rather than an 'upward' movement in the same field.

There is some controversy surrounding the use of _____ to offset economic changes caused by free trade and automation.

a. Retraining
b. BNSF Railway
c. BMC Software, Inc.
d. 3M Company

Chapter 14. Decision Making; Relevant Costs and Benefits

24. _____ is the study of how the variation (uncertainty) in the output of a mathematical model can be apportioned, qualitatively or quantitatively, to different sources of variation in the input of a model.

In more general terms uncertainty and sensitivity analyses investigate the robustness of a study when the study includes some form of mathematical modelling. While uncertainty analysis studies the overall uncertainty in the conclusions of the study, _____ tries to identify what source of uncertainty weights more on the study's conclusions.

- a. Free cash flow
- b. Kaizen
- c. Time to market
- d. Sensitivity analysis

25. _____ is an overall management philosophy introduced by Dr. Eliyahu M. Goldratt in his 1984 book titled The Goal, that is geared to help organizations continually achieve their goal. The title comes from the contention that any manageable system is limited in achieving more of its goal by a very small number of constraints, and that there is always at least one constraint. The _____ process seeks to identify the constraint and restructure the rest of the organization around it, through the use of the Five Focusing Steps.

- a. Six Sigma
- b. Theory of constraints
- c. Lean manufacturing
- d. Lean production

26. _____ is a term used in subtly different ways in a number of fields, including philosophy, physics, statistics, economics, finance, insurance, psychology, sociology, engineering, and information science. It applies to predictions of future events, to physical measurements already made, or to the unknown.

In his seminal work Risk, _____, and Profit University of Chicago economist Frank Knight (1921) established the important distinction between risk and _____:

'_____ must be taken in a sense radically distinct from the familiar notion of risk, from which it has never been properly separated....

- a. ABC Television Network
- b. AMEX
- c. AIG
- d. Uncertainty

27. Just in Time could refer to the following:

- _____, an inventory strategy that reduces in-process inventory
- _____ compilation, a technique for improving the performance of bytecode-compiled programming systems

- a. Just-in-time
- b. Help desk and incident reporting auditing
- c. Comparable
- d. Fiscal

Chapter 14. Decision Making; Relevant Costs and Benefits

28. _____ is the balance of the amounts of cash being received and paid by a business during a defined period of time, sometimes tied to a specific project. Measurement of _____ can be used

- to evaluate the state or performance of a business or project.
- to determine problems with liquidity. Being profitable does not necessarily mean being liquid. A company can fail because of a shortage of cash, even while profitable.
- to project rate of returns. The time of _____s into and out of projects are used as inputs to financial models such as internal rate of return, and net present value.
- to examine income or growth of a business when it is believed that accrual accounting concepts do not represent economic realities. Alternately, _____ can be used to 'validate' the net income generated by accrual accounting.

_____ as a generic term may be used differently depending on context, and certain _____ definitions may be adapted by analysts and users for their own uses. Common terms include operating _____ and free _____.

a. Flow-through entity
b. Cash flow
c. Controlling interest
d. Commercial paper

29. _____ is the calculated approximation of a result which is usable even if input data may be incomplete or uncertain.

In statistics, see _____ theory, estimator.

In mathematics, approximation or _____ typically means finding upper or lower bounds of a quantity that cannot readily be computed precisely and is also an educated guess .

a. AIG
b. Estimation
c. AMEX
d. ABC Television Network

30. In economics and sociology, an _____ is any factor (financial or non-financial) that enables or motivates a particular course of action, or counts as a reason for preferring one choice to the alternatives. It is an expectation that encourages people to behave in a certain way. Since human beings are purposeful creatures, the study of _____ structures is central to the study of all economic activity (both in terms of individual decision-making and in terms of co-operation and competition within a larger institutional structure.)

a. ABC Television Network
b. AIG
c. Incentive
d. AMEX

31. _____ is the process whereby an organization establishes the parameters within which programs, investments, and acquisitions are reaching the desired results. Performance Reference Model of the Federal Enterprise Architecture, 2005.

This process of measuring performance often requires the use of statistical evidence to determine progress toward specific defined organizational objectives.

There are many types of measurements.

a. Management by objectives
c. Trustee
b. Performance measurement
d. Management by exception

32. _____ is systematic determination of merit, worth, and significance of something or someone using criteria against a set of standards. _____ often is used to characterize and appraise subjects of interest in a wide range of human enterprises, including the arts, criminal justice, foundations and non-profit organizations, government, health care, and other human services.

Depending on the topic of interest, there are professional groups which look to the quality and rigor of the _____ process.

a. AMEX
c. Evaluation
b. ABC Television Network
d. AIG

33. In economics, _____ or _____ goods or real _____ refers to factors of production used to create goods or services that are not themselves significantly consumed (though they may depreciate) in the production process. _____ goods may be acquired with money or financial _____. In finance and accounting, _____ generally refers to financial wealth, especially that used to start or maintain a business.

a. Vyborg Appeal
c. Capital
b. Disclosure
d. Screening

34. _____ is the planning process used to determine whether a firm's long term investments such as new machinery, replacement machinery, new plants, new products, and research development projects are worth pursuing. It is budget for major capital, or investment, expenditures.

Many formal methods are used in _____, including the techniques such as

- Net present value
- Profitability index
- Internal rate of return
- Modified Internal Rate of Return
- Equivalent annuity

These methods use the incremental cash flows from each potential investment, or project. Techniques based on accounting earnings and accounting rules are sometimes used - though economists consider this to be improper - such as the accounting rate of return, and 'return on investment.' Simplified and hybrid methods are used as well, such as payback period and discounted payback period.

a. Gross profit
c. Cash flow
b. Capital budgeting
d. Preferred stock

35. In economic models, the _____ time frame assumes no fixed factors of production. Firms can enter or leave the marketplace, and the cost (and availability) of land, labor, raw materials, and capital goods can be assumed to vary. In contrast, in the short-run time frame, certain factors are assumed to be fixed, because there is not sufficient time for them to change.

Chapter 14. Decision Making; Relevant Costs and Benefits

a. 3M Company
b. BMC Software, Inc.
c. Short-run
d. Long-run

36. In economics, the concept of the _____ refers to the decision-making time frame of a firm in which at least one factor of production is fixed. Costs which are fixed in the _____ have no impact on a firms decisions. For example a firm can raise output by increasing the amount of labour through overtime.

a. Long-run
b. 3M Company
c. BMC Software, Inc.
d. Short-run

37. Simply put, _____ is the value of money figuring in a given amount of interest for a given amount of time. For example 100 dollars of todays money held for a year at 5 percent interest is worth 105 dollars, therefore 100 dollars paid now or 105 dollars paid exactly one year from now is the same amount of payment of money with that given intersest at that given amount of time. This notion dates at least to Martín de Azpilcueta of the School of Salamanca.

a. Competition law
b. Collusion
c. Merck ' Co., Inc.
d. Time value of money

38. In economics, _____ are business expenses that are not dependent on the activities of the business They tend to be time-related, such as salaries or rents being paid per month. This is in contrast to variable costs, which are volume-related (and are paid per quantity.)

In management accounting, _____ are defined as expenses that do not change in proportion to the activity of a business, within the relevant period or scale of production.

a. Fixed costs
b. Marginal cost
c. Cost accounting
d. Cost of quality

39. In optimization (a branch of mathematics), a candidate solution is a member of a set of possible solutions to a given problem. A candidate solution does not have to be a likely or reasonable solution to the problem. The space of all candidate solutions is called the _____, feasible set, search space, or solution space.

a. 3M Company
b. BMC Software, Inc.
c. BNSF Railway
d. Feasible region

40. In mathematical optimization theory, the _____, created by the American mathematician George Dantzig in 1947, is a popular algorithm for numerical solution of the linear programming problem. The journal Computing in Science and Engineering listed it as one of the top 10 algorithms of the century.

An unrelated, but similarly named method is the Nelder-Mead method or downhill simplex method due to Nelder ' Mead (1965) and is a numerical method for optimizing many-dimensional unconstrained problems, belonging to the more general class of search algorithms.

a. 3M Company
b. BMC Software, Inc.
c. BNSF Railway
d. Simplex algorithm

41. An _____ is a practitioner of accountancy, which is the measurement, disclosure or provision of assurance about financial information that helps managers, investors, tax authorities and other decision makers make resource allocation decisions.

The word '_____' is derived from the French 'Compter' which took its origin from the Latin 'Computare'. The word was formerly written in English as 'Accomptant', but in process of time the word, which was always pronounced by dropping the 'p', became gradually changed both in pronunciation and in orthography to its present form.

a. ABC Television Network
c. AIG

b. AMEX
d. Accountant

Chapter 15. Target Costing and Cost Analysis for Pricing Decisions

1. _____ is one of the four Ps of the marketing mix. The other three aspects are product, promotion, and place. It is also a key variable in microeconomic price allocation theory.
   a. Target costing
   b. Pricing
   c. Price
   d. Cost-plus pricing

2. A _____ is any one of a variety of different systems, institutions, procedures, social relations and infrastructures whereby persons trade, and goods and services are exchanged, forming part of the economy. It is an arrangement that allows buyers and sellers to exchange things. _____s vary in size, range, geographic scale, location, types and variety of human communities, as well as the types of goods and services traded.
   a. Market Failure
   b. Recession
   c. Perfect competition
   d. Market

3. _____ is an economic concept with commonplace familiarity. It is the price that a good or service is offered at, or will fetch, in the marketplace. It is of interest mainly in the study of microeconomics.
   a. Financial instruments
   b. Transfer agent
   c. Spot rate
   d. Market price

4. Total _____ is a method of Accounting cost which entails the full cost of manufacturing or providing a service. This includes not just the costs of materials and labour, but also of all manufacturing overheads (whether e;fixede; or e;variablee;.) One of the main reasons for absorbing overheads into the cost of units is for inventory valuation purposes.
   a. ABC Television Network
   b. AIG
   c. AMEX
   d. Absorption costing

5. _____ is the process of comparing the cost, cycle time, productivity, or quality of a specific process or method to another that is widely considered to be an industry standard or best practice. Essentially, _____ provides a snapshot of the performance of your business and helps you understand where you are in relation to a particular standard. The result is often a business case for making changes in order to make improvements.
   a. BMC Software, Inc.
   b. Strategic business unit
   c. 3M Company
   d. Benchmarking

6. _____ in economics and business is the result of an exchange and from that trade we assign a numerical monetary value to a good, service or asset. If Alice trades Bob 4 apples for an orange, the _____ of an orange is 4 apples. Inversely, the _____ of an apple is 1/4 oranges.
   a. Price discrimination
   b. Transactional Net Margin Method
   c. Discounts and allowances
   d. Price

7. _____, in managerial economics is a form of cost accounting. It is a simplified model, useful for elementary instruction and for short-run decisions.

Cost-volume-profit (CVP) analysis expands the use of information provided by breakeven analysis.

   a. Fixed costs
   b. Cost of quality
   c. Cost-volume-profit analysis
   d. Cost accounting

8. In economics, the _____ can be defined as the graph depicting the relationship between the price of a certain commodity, and the amount of it that consumers are willing and able to purchase at that given price. It is a graphic representation of a demand schedule. The _____ for all consumers together follows from the _____ of every individual consumer: the individual demands at each price are added together.
   a. Demand curve
   b. P/E ratio
   c. Moving average
   d. Chief executive officer

9. In economics and finance, _____ is the change in total cost that arises when the quantity produced changes by one unit. It is the cost of producing one more unit of a good. Mathematically, the _____ function is expressed as the first derivative of the total cost (TC) function with respect to quantity (Q.)
   a. Marginal cost
   b. Cost accounting
   c. Cost of quality
   d. Variable cost

10. In economics, and cost accounting, _____ describes the total economic cost of production and is made up of variable costs, which vary according to the quantity of a good produced and include inputs such as labor and raw materials, plus fixed costs, which are independent of the quantity of a good produced and include inputs (capital) that cannot be varied in the short term, such as buildings and machinery. _____ in economics includes the total opportunity cost of each factor of production in addition to fixed and variable costs.

The rate at which _____ changes as the amount produced changes is called marginal cost.

   a. Total cost
   b. 3M Company
   c. BNSF Railway
   d. BMC Software, Inc.

11. In economics, business, retail, and accounting, a _____ is the value of money that has been used up to produce something, and hence is not available for use anymore. In economics, a _____ is an alternative that is given up as a result of a decision. In business, the _____ may be one of acquisition, in which case the amount of money expended to acquire it is counted as _____.
   a. Prime cost
   b. Cost of quality
   c. Cost allocation
   d. Cost

12. In probability theory and statistics, the _____ of a random variable, probability distribution averaging the squared distance of its possible values from the expected value (mean.) Whereas the mean is a way to describe the location of a distribution, the _____ is a way to capture its scale or degree of being spread out. The unit of _____ is the square of the unit of the original variable.
   a. Variance
   b. Time series
   c. Statistics
   d. Monte Carlo methods

13. In economics, _____ is the ratio of the percent change in one variable to the percent change in another variable. It is a tool for measuring the responsiveness of a function to changes in parameters in a relative way. Commonly analyzed are _____ of substitution, price and wealth.
   a. Elasticity
   b. Economic value added
   c. Old Navy
   d. U-Haul

Chapter 15. Target Costing and Cost Analysis for Pricing Decisions

14. _____ is a pricing method used by companies. It is used primarily because it is easy to calculate and requires little information. There are several varieties, but the common thread in all of them is that one first calculates the cost of the product, then includes an additional amount to represent profit.
   a. Price discrimination
   b. Target costing
   c. Penetration pricing
   d. Cost-plus pricing

15. _____ is the difference between the cost of a good or service and its selling price. A _____ is added on to the total cost incurred by the producer of a good or service in order to create a profit. The total cost reflects the total amount of both fixed and variable expenses to produce and distribute a product.
   a. Merck ' Co., Inc.
   b. Statements of Financial Accounting Standards No. 133, Accounting for Derivative Instruments and Hedging Activities
   c. Corporate Bond
   d. Markup

16. _____s are expenses that change in proportion to the activity of a business. In other words, _____ is the sum of marginal costs. It can also be considered normal costs.
   a. Variable cost
   b. Quality costs
   c. Fixed costs
   d. Cost accounting

17. _____ is the pricing technique of setting a relatively low initial entry price, often lower than the eventual market price, to attract new customers. The strategy works on the expectation that customers will switch to the new brand because of the lower price. _____ is most commonly associated with a marketing objective of increasing market share or sales volume, rather than to make profit in the short term.
   a. Price
   b. Transactional Net Margin Method
   c. Penetration pricing
   d. Transfer pricing

18. _____ is a costing model that identifies activities in an organization and assigns the cost of each activity resource to all products and services according to the actual consumption by each: it assigns more indirect costs (overhead) into direct costs.

In this way an organization can establish the true cost of its individual products and services for the purposes of identifying and eliminating those which are unprofitable and lowering the prices of those which are overpriced.

In a business organization, the ABC methodology assigns an organization's resource costs through activities to the products and services provided to its customers.

   a. ABC Television Network
   b. Activity-based management
   c. Indirect costs
   d. Activity-based costing

19. In engineering and manufacturing, _____ and quality engineering are used in developing systems to ensure products or services are designed and produced to meet or exceed customer requirements. Refer to the definition by Merriam-Webster for further information . These systems are often developed in conjunction with other business and engineering disciplines using a cross-functional approach.
   a. BMC Software, Inc.
   b. BNSF Railway
   c. Quality control
   d. 3M Company

Chapter 15. Target Costing and Cost Analysis for Pricing Decisions

20. _____ is a pricing method used by firms. It is defined as 'a cost management tool for reducing the overall cost of a product over its entire life-cycle with the help of production, engineering, research and design'. A target cost is the maximum amount of cost that can be incurred on a product and with it the firm can still earn the required profit margin from that product at a particular selling price.
   a. Target costing
   b. Penetration pricing
   c. Pricing
   d. Discounts and allowances

21. _____, commonly known as e-commerce or eCommerce, consists of the buying and selling of products or services over electronic systems such as the Internet and other computer networks. The amount of trade conducted electronically has grown extraordinarily since the spread of the Internet. A wide variety of commerce is conducted in this way, spurring and drawing on innovations in electronic funds transfer, supply chain management, Internet marketing, online transaction processing, electronic data interchange (EDI), inventory management systems, and automated data collection systems.
   a. ABC Television Network
   b. AIG
   c. Electronic data interchange
   d. Electronic commerce

22. A _____ is a group of employees from various functional areas of the organization - research, engineering, marketing, finance. human resources, and operations, for example - who are all focused on a specific objective and are responsible to work as a team to improve coordination and innovation across divisions and resolve mutual problems.
   a. BNSF Railway
   b. 3M Company
   c. Cross-functional team
   d. BMC Software, Inc.

23. A _____, also client, buyer or purchaser is the buyer or user of the paid products of an individual or organization, mostly called the supplier or seller. This is typically through purchasing or renting goods or services.
   a. BMC Software, Inc.
   b. BNSF Railway
   c. 3M Company
   d. Customer

24. The _____ is used for the design, development, analysis, and optimization of technical processes and is mainly applied to chemical plants and chemical processes, but also to power stations, and similar technical facilities. Process flow diagram of a typical amine treating process used in industrial plants

The _____ is a model-based representation of chemical, physical, biological, and other technical processes and unit operations in software. Basic prerequisites are a thorough knowledge of chemical and physical properties of pure components and mixtures, of reactions, and of mathematical models which, in combination, allow the calculation of a process in computers.

   a. BNSF Railway
   b. 3M Company
   c. Process simulation
   d. BMC Software, Inc.

25. _____ can be defined as the idea generation, concept development, testing and manufacturing or implementation of a physical object or service. _____ers conceptualize and evaluate ideas, making them tangible through products in a more systematic approach. The role of a _____er encompasses many characteristics of the marketing manager, product manager, industrial designer and design engineer.
   a. Product design
   b. Arthur Betz Laffer
   c. Abby Joseph Cohen
   d. Alan Greenspan

Chapter 15. Target Costing and Cost Analysis for Pricing Decisions

26. _____ Management is the succession of strategies used by management as a product goes through its _____. The conditions in which a product is sold changes over time and must be managed as it moves through its succession of stages.

The _____ goes through many phases, involves many professional disciplines, and requires many skills, tools and processes.

a. Product life cycle
b. Safety stock
c. Kaizen
d. Procurement

27. _____ in engineering is a method of manufacturing in which the entire production process is controlled by computer. The traditional separated process methods are joined through a computer by CIM. This integration allows that the processes exchange information with each other and they are able to initiate actions.

a. 3M Company
b. BMC Software, Inc.
c. BNSF Railway
d. Computer-integrated manufacturing

28. Just in Time could refer to the following:

- _____, an inventory strategy that reduces in-process inventory
- _____ compilation, a technique for improving the performance of bytecode-compiled programming systems

a. Help desk and incident reporting auditing
b. Comparable
c. Fiscal
d. Just-in-time

29. _____ is concerned with the provisions and use of accounting information to managers within organizations, to provide them with the basis to make informed business decisions that will allow them to be better equipped in their management and control functions.

In contrast to financial accountancy information, _____ information is:

- usually confidential and used by management, instead of publicly reported;
- forward-looking, instead of historical;
- pragmatically computed using extensive management information systems and internal controls, instead of complying with accounting standards.

This is because of the different emphasis: _____ information is used within an organization, typically for decision-making.

a. Nonassurance services
b. Grenzplankostenrechnung
c. Governmental accounting
d. Management accounting

30. The _____ is a concept from business management that was first described and popularized by Michael Porter in his 1985 best-seller, Competitive Advantage: Creating and Sustaining Superior Performance.

Chapter 15. Target Costing and Cost Analysis for Pricing Decisions

A _____ is a chain of activities. Products pass through all activities of the chain in order and at each activity the product gains some value.

   a. Customer relationship management   b. Product differentiation
   c. Market segmentation   d. Value chain

31. _____ is the balance of the amounts of cash being received and paid by a business during a defined period of time, sometimes tied to a specific project. Measurement of _____ can be used

- to evaluate the state or performance of a business or project.
- to determine problems with liquidity. Being profitable does not necessarily mean being liquid. A company can fail because of a shortage of cash, even while profitable.
- to project rate of returns. The time of _____s into and out of projects are used as inputs to financial models such as internal rate of return, and net present value.
- to examine income or growth of a business when it is believed that accrual accounting concepts do not represent economic realities. Alternately, _____ can be used to 'validate' the net income generated by accrual accounting.

_____ as a generic term may be used differently depending on context, and certain _____ definitions may be adapted by analysts and users for their own uses. Common terms include operating _____ and free _____.

   a. Commercial paper   b. Flow-through entity
   c. Controlling interest   d. Cash flow

32. _____ is the calculated approximation of a result which is usable even if input data may be incomplete or uncertain.

In statistics, see _____ theory, estimator.

In mathematics, approximation or _____ typically means finding upper or lower bounds of a quantity that cannot readily be computed precisely and is also an educated guess .

   a. AIG   b. ABC Television Network
   c. Estimation   d. AMEX

33. _____ is a systematic method to improve the 'value' of goods or products and services by using an examination of function. Value, as defined, is the ratio of function to cost. Value can therefore be increased by either improving the function or reducing the cost.

   a. Productivity   b. Changeover
   c. Value engineering   d. Deming Prize

34. _____ are costs that are not directly accountable to a particular function or product. _____ may be either fixed or variable. _____ include taxes, administration, personnel and security costs, and are also known as overhead.

Chapter 15. Target Costing and Cost Analysis for Pricing Decisions

a. Activity-based costing
b. Indirect costs
c. ABC Television Network
d. Activity-based management

35. In finance, _____ also known as return on investment, rate of profit or sometimes just return, is the ratio of money gained or lost on an investment relative to the amount of money invested. The amount of money gained or lost may be referred to as interest, profit/loss, gain/loss, or net income/loss. The money invested may be referred to as the asset, capital, principal, or the cost basis of the investment.

a. Capital employed
b. Debt to capital ratio
c. Rate of return
d. Theoretical ex-rights price

36. _____ is the acquisition of goods and/or services at the best possible total cost of ownership, in the right quantity and quality, at the right time, in the right place and from the right source for the direct benefit or use of corporations or individuals, generally via a contract. Simple _____ may involve nothing more than repeat purchasing. Complex _____ could involve finding long term partners - or even 'co-destiny' suppliers that might fundamentally commit one organization to another.

a. Procurement
b. Free cash flow
c. Customer satisfaction
d. Time to market

37. _____ is a concept in economics which refers to the extent to which an enterprise or a nation actually uses its installed productive capacity. Thus, it refers to the relationship between actual output that 'is' produced with the installed equipment and the potential output which 'could' be produced with it, if capacity was fully used.

If market demand grows, _____ will rise.

a. BMC Software, Inc.
b. 3M Company
c. Capacity utilization
d. Long-run

38. _____, known in the United States as antitrust law, has three main elements:

- prohibiting agreements or practices that restrict free trading and competition between business entities. This includes in particular the repression of cartels.
- banning abusive behaviour by a firm dominating a market, or anti-competitive practices that tend to lead to such a dominant position. Practices controlled in this way may include predatory pricing, tying, price gouging, refusal to deal, and many others.
- supervising the mergers and acquisitions of large corporations, including some joint ventures. Transactions that are considered to threaten the competitive process can be prohibited altogether, or approved subject to 'remedies' such as an obligation to divest part of the merged business or to offer licences or access to facilities to enable other businesses to continue competing.

The substance and practice of _____ varies from jurisdiction to jurisdiction. Protecting the interests of consumers (consumer welfare) and ensuring that entrepreneurs have an opportunity to compete in the market economy are often treated as important objectives. _____ is closely connected with law on deregulation of access to markets, state aids and subsidies, the privatisation of state owned assets and the establishment of independent sector regulators. In recent decades, _____ has been viewed as a way to provide better public services.

a. Malpractice
b. Competition law
c. Hospital Survey and Construction Act
d. Lease

39. _____ is the practice of selling a product or service at a very low price, intending to drive competitors out of the market, or create barriers to entry for potential new competitors. If competitors or potential competitors cannot sustain equal or lower prices without losing money, they go out of business or choose not to enter the business. The predatory merchant then has fewer competitors or is even a de facto monopoly, and can then raise prices above what the market would otherwise bear.
a. Predatory pricing
b. BMC Software, Inc.
c. BNSF Railway
d. 3M Company

40. _____ exists when sales of identical goods or services are transacted at different prices from the same provider. In a theoretical market with perfect information, no transaction costs or prohibition on secondary exchange (or re-selling) to prevent arbitrage, _____ can only be a feature of monopoly and oligopoly markets, where market power can be exercised. Otherwise, the moment the seller tries to sell the same good at different prices, the buyer at the lower price can arbitrage by selling to the consumer buying at the higher price but with a tiny discount.
a. Price
b. Price discrimination
c. Transactional Net Margin Method
d. Resale price maintenance

41. The _____ of 1936 (or Anti-Price Discrimination Act, 15 U.S.C. § 13) is a United States federal law that prohibits what were considered, at the time of passage, to be anticompetitive practices by producers, specifically price discrimination. It grew out of practices in which chain stores were allowed to purchase goods at lower prices than other retailers.
a. Lien
b. Limited liability
c. Robinson-Patman Act
d. Consumer protection laws

Chapter 16. Capital Expenditure Decisions

1. _____ is one of the four Ps of the marketing mix. The other three aspects are product, promotion, and place. It is also a key variable in microeconomic price allocation theory.
   a. Price
   b. Cost-plus pricing
   c. Pricing
   d. Target costing

2. _____ or net present worth (NPW) is defined as the total present value (PV) of a time series of cash flows. It is a standard method for using the time value of money to appraise long-term projects. Used for capital budgeting, and widely throughout economics, it measures the excess or shortfall of cash flows, in present value terms, once financing charges are met.
   a. Net present value
   b. Future value
   c. 3M Company
   d. Present value

3. In economics, _____ or _____ goods or real _____ refers to factors of production used to create goods or services that are not themselves significantly consumed (though they may depreciate) in the production process. _____ goods may be acquired with money or financial _____. In finance and accounting, _____ generally refers to financial wealth, especially that used to start or maintain a business.
   a. Disclosure
   b. Capital
   c. Screening
   d. Vyborg Appeal

4. In economics, business, retail, and accounting, a _____ is the value of money that has been used up to produce something, and hence is not available for use anymore. In economics, a _____ is an alternative that is given up as a result of a decision. In business, the _____ may be one of acquisition, in which case the amount of money expended to acquire it is counted as _____.
   a. Cost
   b. Cost allocation
   c. Prime cost
   d. Cost of quality

5. The _____ is an expected return that the provider of capital plans to earn on their investment.

   Capital (money) used for funding a business should earn returns for the capital providers who risk their capital. For an investment to be worthwhile, the expected return on capital must be greater than the _____.

   a. Capital flight
   b. 3M Company
   c. BMC Software, Inc.
   d. Cost of capital

6. _____ is the value on a given date of a future payment or series of future payments, discounted to reflect the time value of money and other factors such as investment risk. _____ calculations are widely used in business and economics to provide a means to compare cash flows at different times on a meaningful 'like to like' basis.

   The most commonly applied model of the time value of money is compound interest.

   a. Net present value
   b. 3M Company
   c. Future value
   d. Present value

Chapter 16. Capital Expenditure Decisions

7. An _____ is a term used in behavioral economics to describe those types of behaviors that impose costs on a person in the long-run that are not taken into account when making decisions in the present. Classical Economics discourages government from creating legislation that targets internalities, because it is assumed that the consumer takes these personal costs into account when paying for the good that causes the _____. For example, cigarettes should be taxed because of the negative consumption externalities that they impose, such as second-hand smoke, not because the smoker harms him or herself by smoking.

    a. Operating budget   b. Authorised capital
    c. Inventory turnover ratio   d. Internality

8. The _____ is a capital budgeting metric used by firms to decide whether they should make investments. It is also called discounted cash flow rate of return (DCFROR) or rate of return (ROR.) It is an indicator of the efficiency or quality of an investment, as opposed to net present value (NPV), which indicates value or magnitude.

    a. AIG   b. ABC Television Network
    c. AMEX   d. Internal rate of return

9. In finance, _____ also known as return on investment, rate of profit or sometimes just return, is the ratio of money gained or lost on an investment relative to the amount of money invested. The amount of money gained or lost may be referred to as interest, profit/loss, gain/loss, or net income/loss. The money invested may be referred to as the asset, capital, principal, or the cost basis of the investment.

    a. Debt to capital ratio   b. Rate of return
    c. Theoretical ex-rights price   d. Capital employed

10. _____ is the balance of the amounts of cash being received and paid by a business during a defined period of time, sometimes tied to a specific project. Measurement of _____ can be used

- to evaluate the state or performance of a business or project.
- to determine problems with liquidity. Being profitable does not necessarily mean being liquid. A company can fail because of a shortage of cash, even while profitable.
- to project rate of returns. The time of _____s into and out of projects are used as inputs to financial models such as internal rate of return, and net present value.
- to examine income or growth of a business when it is believed that accrual accounting concepts do not represent economic realities. Alternately, _____ can be used to 'validate' the net income generated by accrual accounting.

_____ as a generic term may be used differently depending on context, and certain _____ definitions may be adapted by analysts and users for their own uses. Common terms include operating _____ and free _____.

    a. Cash flow   b. Controlling interest
    c. Commercial paper   d. Flow-through entity

11. _____ are made by investors and investment managers.

Investors commonly perform investment analysis by making use of fundamental analysis, technical analysis and gut feel.

_____ are often supported by decision tools.

Chapter 16. Capital Expenditure Decisions 113

a. AIG
c. ABC Television Network

b. Incremental capital-output ratio
d. Investment decisions

12. _____ is a term used in accounting, economics and finance to spread the cost of an asset over the span of several years.

In simple words we can say that _____ is the reduction in the value of an asset due to usage, passage of time, wear and tear, technological outdating or obsolescence, depletion, inadequacy, rot, rust, decay or other such factors.

In accounting, _____ is a term used to describe any method of attributing the historical or purchase cost of an asset across its useful life, roughly corresponding to normal wear and tear.

a. Net profit
c. Current asset

b. General ledger
d. Depreciation

13. In physics, and more specifically kinematics, _____ is the change in velocity over time. Because velocity is a vector, it can change in two ways: a change in magnitude and/or a change in direction. In one dimension, _____ is the rate at which something speeds up or slows down.

a. AMEX
c. Acceleration

b. AIG
d. ABC Television Network

14. In business and accounting, _____ are everything of value that is owned by a person or company. It is a claim on the property your income of a borrower. The balance sheet of a firm records the monetary value of the _____ owned by the firm.

a. Accrual basis accounting

c. Accounts receivable

b. Assets

d. Earnings before interest, taxes, depreciation and amortization

15. _____ is concerned with the provisions and use of accounting information to managers within organizations, to provide them with the basis to make informed business decisions that will allow them to be better equipped in their management and control functions.

In contrast to financial accountancy information, _____ information is:

- usually confidential and used by management, instead of publicly reported;
- forward-looking, instead of historical;
- pragmatically computed using extensive management information systems and internal controls, instead of complying with accounting standards.

This is because of the different emphasis: _____ information is used within an organization, typically for decision-making.

a. Nonassurance services
b. Grenzplankostenrechnung
c. Management accounting
d. Governmental accounting

16. An _____ is a tax levied on the financial income of people, corporations, or other legal entities. Various _____ systems exist, with varying degrees of tax incidence. Income taxation can be progressive, proportional, or regressive.
   a. Implied level of government service
   b. Income tax
   c. Individual Retirement Arrangement
   d. Ordinary income

17. _____ refers to any one of several methods by which a company, for 'financial accounting' and/or tax purposes, depreciates a fixed asset in such a way that the amount of depreciation taken each year is higher during the earlier years of an assete;s life. For financial accounting purposes, _____ is generally used when an asset is expected to be much more productive during its early years, so that depreciation expense will more accurately represent how much of an assete;s usefulness is being used up each year. For tax purposes, _____ provides a way of deferring corporate income taxes by reducing taxable income in current years, in exchange for increased taxable income in future years.
   a. Indirect tax
   b. Effective marginal tax rates
   c. Accelerated depreciation
   d. User charge

18. In finance, an _____ is a contract between a buyer and a seller that gives the buyer the right--but not the obligation-- to buy or to sell a particular asset (the underlying asset) at a later time at an agreed price. In return for granting the _____, the seller collects a payment (the premium) from the buyer. A call _____ gives the buyer the right to buy the underlying asset; a put _____ gives the buyer of the _____ the right to sell the underlying asset.
   a. ABC Television Network
   b. AMEX
   c. AIG
   d. Option

19. In accounting, _____ has a very specific meaning. It is an outflow of cash or other valuable assets from a person or company to another person or company. This outflow of cash is generally one side of a trade for products or services that have equal or better current or future value to the buyer than to the seller.
   a. AIG
   b. ABC Television Network
   c. AMEX
   d. Expense

20. A _____ is the pinnacle activity involved in selling products or services in return for money or other compensation. It is an act of completion of a commercial activity.

A _____ is completed by the seller, the owner of the goods.

   a. High yield stock
   b. Maturity
   c. Tertiary sector of economy
   d. Sale

21. _____ is a company's financial statement that indicates how the revenue is transformed into the net income The purpose of the _____ is to show managers and investors whether the company made or lost money during the period being reported.

The important thing to remember about an _____ is that it represents a period of time.

Chapter 16. Capital Expenditure Decisions

a. AMEX
c. ABC Television Network
b. AIG
d. Income statement

22. In economics, _____ is a rise in the general level of prices of goods and services in an economy over a period of time. When the general price level rises, each unit of currency buys fewer goods and services; consequently, _____ is also a decline in the real value of money--a loss of purchasing power in the medium of exchange which is also the monetary unit of account in the economy. A chief measure of general price-level _____ is the general _____ rate, which is the percentage change in a general price index (normally the Consumer Price Index) over time.

a. Inflation
c. AIG
b. Opportunity cost
d. ABC Television Network

23. A _____ or a tax-deductible expense affects a taxpayer's income tax. A _____ represents an expense incurred by a taxpayer. They are variable amounts that you can subtract, or deduct, from your gross income. It is subtracted from gross income when the taxpayer computes his or her income taxes.

a. Tax avoidance
c. Tax incidence
b. Tax protester constitutional arguments
d. Tax deduction

24. _____ is an area of engineering practice concerned with the 'application of scientific principles and techniques to problems of cost estimating, cost control, business planning and management science, profitability analysis, project management, and planning and scheduling.'

Key objectives of _____ are to arrive at accurate cost estimates and to avoid cost overruns. The broad array of _____ topics represent the intersection of the fields of project management, business management, and engineering. Most people have a limited view of what engineering encompasses.

a. BNSF Railway
c. 3M Company
b. BMC Software, Inc.
d. Cost engineering

25. _____ is the calculated approximation of a result which is usable even if input data may be incomplete or uncertain.

In statistics, see _____ theory, estimator.

In mathematics, approximation or _____ typically means finding upper or lower bounds of a quantity that cannot readily be computed precisely and is also an educated guess.

a. ABC Television Network
c. AIG
b. AMEX
d. Estimation

26. The _____ is the current method of accelerated asset depreciation required by the United States income tax code. Under _____, all assets are divided into classes which dictate the number of years over which an asset's cost will be recovered.

Prior to the Accelerated Cost Recovery System (ACRS), most capital purchases were depreciated using a straight line technique, that allowed for the depreciation of the asset over its useful life.

a. Modified Accelerated Cost Recovery System
b. BMC Software, Inc.
c. Categorical grants
d. 3M Company

27. _____ is the process of changing the way taxes are collected or managed by the government.

_____ers have different goals. Some seek to reduce the level of taxation of all people by the government.

a. Tax investigation
b. Tax exporting
c. Tax Reform
d. Franchise tax

28. In tax accounting the _____ is the default applicable convention used for federal income tax purposes. Like other conventions, the _____ affects the depreciation deduction computation in the year in which the property is placed into service. Using the _____, a taxpayer claims a half of a year's depreciation for the first taxable year, regardless of when the property was actually put into service.

a. Taxable income
b. Revenue Procedures
c. Reverse Morris trust
d. Half-year convention

29. The term _____ describes two different concepts:

- The first is a recognition of partial payment already made towards taxes due.
- The second is a state benefit paid to workers through the tax system, which has the effect of increasing (rather than reducing) net income.

Within the Australian, Canadian, United Kingdom, and United States tax systems, a _____ is a recognition of partial payment already made towards taxes due. A similar concept exists (fr:Avoir fiscal) in the French tax system. This situation arises, for example, when standard rate tax has been deducted at source , but the tax-payer is subject to further taxation at a higher rate. It also applies in dividend imputation systems.

a. Scientific Research and Experimental Development Tax Incentive Program
b. 3M Company
c. Foreign tax credit
d. Tax credit

30. Straight-line depreciation is the simplest and most often used technique, in which the company estimates the _____ of the asset at the end of the period during which it will be used to generate revenues (useful life), and will expense a portion of original cost in equal increments over that period. The _____ is an estimate of the value of the asset at the time it will be sold or disposed of; it may be zero. _____ is scrap value, by another name.

a. Net profit
b. Generally accepted accounting principles
c. Salvage value
d. Closing entries

31. There are several methods for calculating depreciation, generally based on either the passage of time or the level of activity (or use) of the asset.

_____ is the simplest and most often used technique, in which the company estimates the salvage value of the asset at the end of the period during which it will be used to generate revenues (useful life), and will expense a portion of original cost in equal increments over that period.

Chapter 16. Capital Expenditure Decisions

a. Straight-line depreciation
b. Closing entries
c. Current asset
d. Pro forma

32. In accounting, _____ or carrying value is the value of an asset according to its balance sheet account balance. For assets, the value is based on the original cost of the asset less any depreciation, amortization or impairment costs made against the asset. Traditionally, a company's _____ is its total assets minus intangible assets and liabilities.
   a. Matching principle
   b. Book value
   c. Depreciation
   d. Generally accepted accounting principles

33. _____ is any physical or virtual entity that is owned by an individual or jointly by a group of individuals. An owner of _____ has the right to consume, sell, rent, mortgage, transfer and exchange his or her _____. Important widely-recognized types of _____ include real _____, personal _____ (other physical possessions), and intellectual _____ (rights over artistic creations, inventions, etc.), although the latter is not always as widely recognized or enforced.
   a. Property
   b. Primary authority
   c. Fiduciary
   d. Disclosure requirement

34. _____ is a financial metric which represents operating liquidity available to a business. Along with fixed assets such as plant and equipment, _____ is considered a part of operating capital. It is calculated as current assets minus current liabilities.
   a. 3M Company
   b. BMC Software, Inc.
   c. Working capital management
   d. Working capital

35. _____ identifies the relationship of investment to payoff of a proposed project. The ratio is calculated as follows:

$$\text{Profitability index} = \frac{\text{PV of future cash flows}}{\text{PV of initial investment}}$$

_____ is also known as Profit Investment Ratio, abbreviated to P.I. and Value Investment Ratio (V.I.R.). _____ is a good tool for ranking projects because it allows you to clearly identify the amount of value created per unit of investment, thus if you are capital constrained you wish to invest in those projects which create value most efficiently first.

Nota Bene; Statements below this paragraph assume the cash flow calculated does not include the investment made in the project.

   a. Debt ratio
   b. 3M Company
   c. Finance lease
   d. Profitability index

36. _____ is the planning process used to determine whether a firm's long term investments such as new machinery, replacement machinery, new plants, new products, and research development projects are worth pursuing. It is budget for major capital, or investment, expenditures.

Many formal methods are used in _____, including the techniques such as

- Net present value
- Profitability index
- Internal rate of return
- Modified Internal Rate of Return
- Equivalent annuity

These methods use the incremental cash flows from each potential investment, or project. Techniques based on accounting earnings and accounting rules are sometimes used - though economists consider this to be improper - such as the accounting rate of return, and 'return on investment.' Simplified and hybrid methods are used as well, such as payback period and discounted payback period.

　a. Cash flow
　c. Capital budgeting
　b. Preferred stock
　d. Gross profit

37. _____ in business and economics refers to the period of time required for the return on an investment to 'repay' the sum of the original investment. For example, a $1000 investment which returned $500 per year would have a two year _____. It intuitively measures how long something takes to 'pay for itself.' Shorter _____s are obviously preferable to longer _____s (all else being equal.)

　a. Fair market value
　c. Segregated portfolio company
　b. Net worth
　d. Payback period

38. _____ is a costing model that identifies activities in an organization and assigns the cost of each activity resource to all products and services according to the actual consumption by each: it assigns more indirect costs (overhead) into direct costs.

In this way an organization can establish the true cost of its individual products and services for the purposes of identifying and eliminating those which are unprofitable and lowering the prices of those which are overpriced.

In a business organization, the ABC methodology assigns an organization's resource costs through activities to the products and services provided to its customers.

　a. Activity-based management
　c. Indirect costs
　b. ABC Television Network
　d. Activity-based costing

39. _____ in engineering is a method of manufacturing in which the entire production process is controlled by computer. The traditional separated process methods are joined through a computer by CIM. This integration allows that the processes exchange information with each other and they are able to initiate actions.

　a. 3M Company
　c. BNSF Railway
　b. BMC Software, Inc.
　d. Computer-integrated manufacturing

Chapter 16. Capital Expenditure Decisions

40. Just in Time could refer to the following:

    - _____, an inventory strategy that reduces in-process inventory
    - _____ compilation, a technique for improving the performance of bytecode-compiled programming systems

    a. Comparable
    b. Fiscal
    c. Help desk and incident reporting auditing
    d. Just-in-time

41. The term _____ is used in finance theory to refer to any terminating stream of fixed payments over a specified period of time. This usage is most commonly seen in academic discussions of finance, usually in connection with the valuation of the stream of payments, taking into account time value of money concepts such as interest rate and future value.

    Examples of these are regular deposits to a savings account, monthly home mortgage payments and monthly insurance payments.

    a. Intangible
    b. Improvement
    c. Annuity
    d. Appropriation

42. _____ measures the nominal future sum of money that a given sum of money is 'worth' at a specified time in the future assuming a certain interest rate rate of return; it is the present value multiplied by the accumulation function.

    The value does not include corrections for inflation or other factors that affect the true value of money in the future. This is used in time value of money calculations.

    a. Net present value
    b. Present value
    c. 3M Company
    d. Future value

43. Simply put, _____ is the value of money figuring in a given amount of interest for a given amount of time. For example 100 dollars of todays money held for a year at 5 percent interest is worth 105 dollars, therefore 100 dollars paid now or 105 dollars paid exactly one year from now is the same amount of payment of money with that given intersest at that given amount of time. This notion dates at least to Martín de Azpilcueta of the School of Salamanca.
    a. Collusion
    b. Time value of money
    c. Competition law
    d. Merck ' Co., Inc.

44. An _____ is the price a borrower pays for the use of money they do not own, for instance a small company might borrow from a bank to kick start their business, and the return a lender receives for deferring the use of funds, by lending it to the borrower. _____s are normally expressed as a percentage rate over the period of one year.

    _____s targets are also a vital tool of monetary policy and are used to control variables like investment, inflation, and unemployment.

    a. AIG
    b. ABC Television Network
    c. Interest rate
    d. AMEX

Chapter 16. Capital Expenditure Decisions

45. In economics, _____ refers to any price or value expressed in money of the day, as opposed to real value, which adjusts for the effect of inflation. Examples include a bundle of commodities, such as gross domestic product, and income. For a series of _____s in successive years, different values could be because of differences in the price level, an index of prices.
    a. Nominal value
    b. Market
    c. Recession
    d. Perfect competition

46. In finance and economics _____ or nominal rate of interest refers to the rate of interest before adjustment for inflation (in contrast with the real interest rate); or, for interest rates 'as stated' without adjustment for the full effect of compounding (also referred to as the nominal annual rate.) An interest rate is called nominal if the frequency of compounding (e.g. a month) is not identical to the basic time unit (normally a year.)

The real interest rate includes compensation for the lender's lost value due to inflation, whereas the _____ excludes inflation.

    a. Nominal interest rate
    b. BMC Software, Inc.
    c. BNSF Railway
    d. 3M Company

47. The '_____' is approximately the nominal interest rate minus the inflation rate Since the inflation rate over the course of a loan is not known initially, volatility in inflation represents a risk to both the lender and the borrower.

In economics and finance, an individual who lends money for repayment at a later point in time expects to be compensated for the time value of money, or not having the use of that money while it is lent.

    a. BMC Software, Inc.
    b. BNSF Railway
    c. Real interest rate
    d. 3M Company

48. _____ is the concept of adding accumulated interest back to the principal, so that interest is earned on interest from that moment on. The act of declaring interest to be principal is called compounding (i.e., interest is compounded.) A loan, for example, may have its interest compounded every month: in this case, a loan with $100 principal and 1% interest per month would have a balance of $101 at the end of the first month.
    a. Kanban
    b. Risk management
    c. Compound interest
    d. Trademark

49. _____ is a fee paid on borrowed assets. It is the price paid for the use of borrowed money , or, money earned by deposited funds .Assets that are sometimes lent with _____ include money, shares, consumer goods through hire purchase, major assets such as aircraft, and even entire factories in finance lease arrangements. The _____ is calculated upon the value of the assets in the same manner as upon money.
    a. ABC Television Network
    b. AIG
    c. Insolvency
    d. Interest

Chapter 17. Absorption, Variable, and Throughput Costing

1. _____ is a costing model that identifies activities in an organization and assigns the cost of each activity resource to all products and services according to the actual consumption by each: it assigns more indirect costs (overhead) into direct costs.

In this way an organization can establish the true cost of its individual products and services for the purposes of identifying and eliminating those which are unprofitable and lowering the prices of those which are overpriced.

In a business organization, the ABC methodology assigns an organization's resource costs through activities to the products and services provided to its customers.

   a. ABC Television Network
   b. Activity-based costing
   c. Indirect costs
   d. Activity-based management

2. _____s are expenses that change in proportion to the activity of a business. In other words, _____ is the sum of marginal costs. It can also be considered normal costs.
   a. Quality costs
   b. Cost accounting
   c. Variable cost
   d. Fixed costs

3. Total _____ is a method of Accounting cost which entails the full cost of manufacturing or providing a service. This includes not just the costs of materials and labour, but also of all manufacturing overheads (whether e;fixede; or e;variablee;.) One of the main reasons for absorbing overheads into the cost of units is for inventory valuation purposes.
   a. Absorption costing
   b. AIG
   c. AMEX
   d. ABC Television Network

4. In economics, business, retail, and accounting, a _____ is the value of money that has been used up to produce something, and hence is not available for use anymore. In economics, a _____ is an alternative that is given up as a result of a decision. In business, the _____ may be one of acquisition, in which case the amount of money expended to acquire it is counted as _____.
   a. Cost allocation
   b. Cost of quality
   c. Cost
   d. Prime cost

5. _____, in managerial economics is a form of cost accounting. It is a simplified model, useful for elementary instruction and for short-run decisions.

Cost-volume-profit (CVP) analysis expands the use of information provided by breakeven analysis.

   a. Fixed costs
   b. Cost-volume-profit analysis
   c. Cost accounting
   d. Cost of quality

122 *Chapter 17. Absorption, Variable, and Throughput Costing*

6. A _____ has several related meanings:

   - a daily record of events or business; a private _____ is usually referred to as a diary.
   - a newspaper or other periodical, in the literal sense of one published each day;
   - many publications issued at stated intervals, such as magazines, or scholarly academic _____s, or the record of the transactions of a society, are often called _____s. Although _____ is sometimes used, erroneously, as a synonym for 'magazine,' in academic use, a _____ refers to a serious, scholarly publication, most often peer-reviewed. A non-scholarly magazine written for an educated audience about an industry or an area of professional activity is usually called a professional magazine.

The word 'journalist' for one whose business is writing for the public press has been in use since the end of the 17th century.

Open access _____s are scholarly _____s that are available to the reader without financial or other barrier other than access to the internet itself. Some are subsidized, and some require payment on behalf of the author. Subsidized _____s are financed by an academic institution or a government information center.

   a. 3M Company
   c. BMC Software, Inc.
   b. BNSF Railway
   d. Journal

7. _____ is a company's financial statement that indicates how the revenue is transformed into the net income The purpose of the _____ is to show managers and investors whether the company made or lost money during the period being reported.

The important thing to remember about an _____ is that it represents a period of time.

   a. AMEX
   c. Income statement
   b. ABC Television Network
   d. AIG

8. In economics ' business, specifically cost accounting, the _____ is the point at which cost or expenses and revenue are equal: there is no net loss or gain, and one has 'broken even'. A profit or a loss has not been made, although opportunity costs have been paid, and capital has received the risk-adjusted, expected return.

For example, if the business sells less than 200 tables each month, it will make a loss, if it sells more, it will be a profit.

   a. BMC Software, Inc.
   c. 3M Company
   b. Defined benefit pension plan
   d. Break-even point

9. _____ is systematic determination of merit, worth, and significance of something or someone using criteria against a set of standards. _____ often is used to characterize and appraise subjects of interest in a wide range of human enterprises, including the arts, criminal justice, foundations and non-profit organizations, government, health care, and other human services.

Depending on the topic of interest, there are professional groups which look to the quality and rigor of the _____ process.

a. AMEX
b. ABC Television Network
c. AIG
d. Evaluation

10. _____ in economics and business is the result of an exchange and from that trade we assign a numerical monetary value to a good, service or asset. If Alice trades Bob 4 apples for an orange, the _____ of an orange is 4 apples. Inversely, the _____ of an apple is 1/4 oranges.
   a. Discounts and allowances
   b. Transactional Net Margin Method
   c. Price discrimination
   d. Price

11. _____ is one of the four Ps of the marketing mix. The other three aspects are product, promotion, and place. It is also a key variable in microeconomic price allocation theory.
   a. Target costing
   b. Price
   c. Cost-plus pricing
   d. Pricing

12. In business and accounting, _____ are everything of value that is owned by a person or company. It is a claim on the property your income of a borrower. The balance sheet of a firm records the monetary value of the _____ owned by the firm.
   a. Earnings before interest, taxes, depreciation and amortization
   b. Accounts receivable
   c. Accrual basis accounting
   d. Assets

13. Just in Time could refer to the following:

   • _____, an inventory strategy that reduces in-process inventory
   • _____ compilation, a technique for improving the performance of bytecode-compiled programming systems

   a. Just-in-time
   b. Comparable
   c. Help desk and incident reporting auditing
   d. Fiscal

14. In business, _____, Overhead cost or _____ expense refers to an ongoing expense of operating a business. The term _____ is usually used to group expenses that are necessary to the continued functioning of the business, but do not directly generate profits.

   _____ expenses are all costs on the income statement except for direct labor and direct materials.

   a. Intangible assets
   b. ABC Television Network
   c. AIG
   d. Overhead

15. In probability theory and statistics, the _____ of a random variable, probability distribution averaging the squared distance of its possible values from the expected value (mean.) Whereas the mean is a way to describe the location of a distribution, the _____ is a way to capture its scale or degree of being spread out. The unit of _____ is the square of the unit of the original variable.
   a. Monte Carlo methods
   b. Time series
   c. Variance
   d. Statistics

Chapter 17. Absorption, Variable, and Throughput Costing

16. In statistics, _____ (ANOVA) is a collection of statistical models, and their associated procedures, in which the observed variance is partitioned into components due to different explanatory variables. In its simplest form ANOVA gives a statistical test of whether the means of several groups are all equal, and therefore generalizes Student's two-sample t-test to more than two groups.

There are three conceptual classes of such models:

1. Fixed-effects models assumes that the data came from normal populations which may differ only in their means. (Model 1)
2. Random effects models assume that the data describe a hierarchy of different populations whose differences are constrained by the hierarchy. (Model 2)
3. Mixed-effect models describe situations where both fixed and random effects are present. (Model 3)

In practice, there are several types of ANOVA depending on the number of treatments and the way they are applied to the subjects in the experiment:

- One-way ANOVA is used to test for differences among two or more independent groups. Typically, however, the one-way ANOVA is used to test for differences among at least three groups, since the two-group case can be covered by a T-test (Gossett, 1908.)

a. IMF
b. Intergenerational equity
c. Open database connectivity
d. Analysis of variance

17. In economics and sociology, an _____ is any factor (financial or non-financial) that enables or motivates a particular course of action, or counts as a reason for preferring one choice to the alternatives. It is an expectation that encourages people to behave in a certain way. Since human beings are purposeful creatures, the study of _____ structures is central to the study of all economic activity (both in terms of individual decision-making and in terms of co-operation and competition within a larger institutional structure.)

a. AIG
b. ABC Television Network
c. Incentive
d. AMEX

1. In economics, business, retail, and accounting, a _____ is the value of money that has been used up to produce something, and hence is not available for use anymore. In economics, a _____ is an alternative that is given up as a result of a decision. In business, the _____ may be one of acquisition, in which case the amount of money expended to acquire it is counted as _____.
   a. Cost allocation
   b. Cost
   c. Prime cost
   d. Cost of quality

2. In business, _____, Overhead cost or _____ expense refers to an ongoing expense of operating a business. The term _____ is usually used to group expenses that are necessary to the continued functioning of the business, but do not directly generate profits.

   _____ expenses are all costs on the income statement except for direct labor and direct materials.

   a. Intangible assets
   b. ABC Television Network
   c. Overhead
   d. AIG

3. _____ is a process of attributing cost to particular cost centres. For example the wage of the driver of the purchasing department can be allocated to the purchasing department cost centre. It is not necessary to share the wage cost over several different cost centers.
   a. Cost of quality
   b. Cost accounting
   c. Variable cost
   d. Cost allocation

4. _____s are expenses that change in proportion to the activity of a business. In other words, _____ is the sum of marginal costs. It can also be considered normal costs.
   a. Fixed costs
   b. Quality costs
   c. Cost accounting
   d. Variable cost

5. In economic models, the _____ time frame assumes no fixed factors of production. Firms can enter or leave the marketplace, and the cost (and availability) of land, labor, raw materials, and capital goods can be assumed to vary. In contrast, in the short-run time frame, certain factors are assumed to be fixed, because there is not sufficient time for them to change.
   a. 3M Company
   b. BMC Software, Inc.
   c. Short-run
   d. Long-run

6. In economics, the concept of the _____ refers to the decision-making time frame of a firm in which at least one factor of production is fixed. Costs which are fixed in the _____ have no impact on a firms decisions. For example a firm can raise output by increasing the amount of labour through overtime.
   a. 3M Company
   b. Short-run
   c. BMC Software, Inc.
   d. Long-run

7. _____ is a concept that denotes the precise probability of specific eventualities. Technically, the notion of _____ is independent from the notion of value and, as such, eventualities may have both beneficial and adverse consequences. However, in general usage the convention is to focus only on potential negative impact to some characteristic of value that may arise from a future event.
   a. Risk adjusted return on capital
   b. Discounting
   c. Discount factor
   d. Risk

Chapter 18. Allocation of Support Activity Costs and Joint Costs

8. _____ is a concept in economics, finance, and psychology related to the behaviour of consumers and investors under uncertainty. _____ is the reluctance of a person to accept a bargain with an uncertain payoff rather than another bargain with a more certain, but possibly lower, expected payoff. For example, a risk-averse investor might choose to put his or her money into a bank account with a low but guaranteed interest rate, rather than into a stock that is likely to have high returns, but also has a chance of becoming worthless.
   a. Risk adjusted return on capital
   b. Discount factor
   c. Risk aversion
   d. Risk

9. Project _____ : The project _____ is a prediction of the costs associated with a particular company project. These costs include labor, materials, and other related expenses. The project _____ is often broken down into specific tasks, with task _____ s assigned to each.
   a. BNSF Railway
   b. 3M Company
   c. Budget
   d. BMC Software, Inc.

10. Just in Time could refer to the following:

   • _____, an inventory strategy that reduces in-process inventory
   • _____ compilation, a technique for improving the performance of bytecode-compiled programming systems

   a. Fiscal
   b. Help desk and incident reporting auditing
   c. Comparable
   d. Just-in-time

11. A _____ rocket is a rocket that uses two or more stages, each of which contains its own engines and propellant. A tandem or serial stage is mounted on top of another stage; a parallel stage is attached alongside another stage. The result is effectively two or more rockets stacked on top of or attached next to each other.
   a. BMC Software, Inc.
   b. 3M Company
   c. BNSF Railway
   d. Multistage

12. _____ is a costing model that identifies activities in an organization and assigns the cost of each activity resource to all products and services according to the actual consumption by each: it assigns more indirect costs (overhead) into direct costs.

In this way an organization can establish the true cost of its individual products and services for the purposes of identifying and eliminating those which are unprofitable and lowering the prices of those which are overpriced.

In a business organization, the ABC methodology assigns an organization's resource costs through activities to the products and services provided to its customers.

   a. Activity-based management
   b. ABC Television Network
   c. Indirect costs
   d. Activity-based costing

Chapter 18. Allocation of Support Activity Costs and Joint Costs 127

13. A _____ has several related meanings:

- a daily record of events or business; a private _____ is usually referred to as a diary.
- a newspaper or other periodical, in the literal sense of one published each day;
- many publications issued at stated intervals, such as magazines, or scholarly academic _____s, or the record of the transactions of a society, are often called _____s. Although _____ is sometimes used, erroneously, as a synonym for 'magazine,' in academic use, a _____ refers to a serious, scholarly publication, most often peer-reviewed. A non-scholarly magazine written for an educated audience about an industry or an area of professional activity is usually called a professional magazine.

The word 'journalist' for one whose business is writing for the public press has been in use since the end of the 17th century.

Open access _____s are scholarly _____s that are available to the reader without financial or other barrier other than access to the internet itself. Some are subsidized, and some require payment on behalf of the author. Subsidized _____s are financed by an academic institution or a government information center.

a. BMC Software, Inc.
c. Journal
b. 3M Company
d. BNSF Railway

14. _____ concern the operation of a facility, as opposed to maintenance, supply and distribution, health, and safety, emergency response, human resources, security, information technology and other infrastructural support organizations.

Personnel that make up 'operations' are

- operators
- engineers
- technicians
- management

This is mainly in a manufacturing setting.

a. Trade name
c. Consolidated financial statements
b. Manufacturing operations
d. Realization

Chapter 18. Allocation of Support Activity Costs and Joint Costs

15. A _____ is a secondary or incidental product deriving from a manufacturing process, a chemical reaction or a biochemical pathway, and is not the primary product or service being produced. A _____ can be useful and marketable, or it can have negative ecological impact.

- dried blood and blood meal - from slaughterhouse operations
- chicken _____ meal - clean parts of the carcass of slaughtered chicken, such as necks, feet, undeveloped eggs, and intestines.
- chrome shavings - from a stage of leather manufacture
- collagen and gelatin - from the boiled skin and other parts of slaughtered livestock
- feathers - from poultry processing
    - feather meal - from poultry processing
- lanolin - from the cleaning of wool
- manure - from animal husbandry
- meat and bone meal - from the rendering of animal bones and offal
- poultry byproduct and poultry meal - made from unmarketable poultry bones and offal
- poultry litter - swept from the floors of chicken coops
- whey - from cheese manufacturing
- fetal pigs

- acidulated soap stock - from the refining of vegetable oil
- bran and germ - from the milling of whole grains into refined grains
- brewer's yeast - from ethanol fermentation
- cereal food fines - from breakfast cereal processing
- corn stover - residual plant matter after harvesting of cereals
- distillers grains - from ethanol fermentation
- glycerol - from the production of biodiesel
- grape seed oil - recovered from leftovers of the winemaking process
- molasses - from sugar refining
- orange oil and other citrus oils - recovered from the peels of processed fruit
- pectin - recovered from the remains of processed fruit
- sawdust and bark- from the processing of logs into lumber
- soybean meal - from soybean processing
- straw- from grain harvesting

- asphalt - from the refining of crude oil
- fly ash - from the combustion of coal
- slag - from ore refining
- gypsum - from Flue gas desulfurization
- ash and smoke - from the combustion of fuel
- mineral oil - from refining crude oil to produce gasoline
- salt - from desalination

- sludge - from wastewater treatment

a. BMC Software, Inc.
c. 3M Company
b. BNSF Railway
d. By-product

16. _____ is a method of evaluating an asset's worth when held in inventory, in the field of accounting. _____ is part of the Generally Accepted Accounting Principles that apply to valuing inventory, so as to not overstate or understate the value of inventory goods. Net realisable value is generally equal to the selling price of the inventory goods less the selling costs (completion and disposal).

a. BMC Software, Inc.
c. 3M Company
b. Net realizable value
d. Revenue recognition

17. _____ is the balance of the amounts of cash being received and paid by a business during a defined period of time, sometimes tied to a specific project. Measurement of _____ can be used

- to evaluate the state or performance of a business or project.
- to determine problems with liquidity. Being profitable does not necessarily mean being liquid. A company can fail because of a shortage of cash, even while profitable.
- to project rate of returns. The time of _____s into and out of projects are used as inputs to financial models such as internal rate of return, and net present value.
- to examine income or growth of a business when it is believed that accrual accounting concepts do not represent economic realities. Alternately, _____ can be used to 'validate' the net income generated by accrual accounting.

_____ as a generic term may be used differently depending on context, and certain _____ definitions may be adapted by analysts and users for their own uses. Common terms include operating _____ and free _____.

a. Cash flow
c. Commercial paper
b. Controlling interest
d. Flow-through entity

18. _____ is the concept of adding accumulated interest back to the principal, so that interest is earned on interest from that moment on. The act of declaring interest to be principal is called compounding (i.e., interest is compounded.) A loan, for example, may have its interest compounded every month: in this case, a loan with $100 principal and 1% interest per month would have a balance of $101 at the end of the first month.

a. Compound interest
c. Kanban
b. Risk management
d. Trademark

19. _____ measures the nominal future sum of money that a given sum of money is 'worth' at a specified time in the future assuming a certain interest rate rate of return; it is the present value multiplied by the accumulation function.

The value does not include corrections for inflation or other factors that affect the true value of money in the future. This is used in time value of money calculations.

a. Future value
c. 3M Company
b. Net present value
d. Present value

20. An _____ is the price a borrower pays for the use of money they do not own, for instance a small company might borrow from a bank to kick start their business, and the return a lender receives for deferring the use of funds, by lending it to the borrower. _____s are normally expressed as a percentage rate over the period of one year.

_____s targets are also a vital tool of monetary policy and are used to control variables like investment, inflation, and unemployment.

   a. ABC Television Network
   b. AIG
   c. AMEX
   d. Interest rate

21. Simply put, _____ is the value of money figuring in a given amount of interest for a given amount of time. For example 100 dollars of todays money held for a year at 5 percent interest is worth 105 dollars, therefore 100 dollars paid now or 105 dollars paid exactly one year from now is the same amount of payment of money with that given intersest at that given amount of time. This notion dates at least to Martín de Azpilcueta of the School of Salamanca.
   a. Time value of money
   b. Competition law
   c. Merck ' Co., Inc.
   d. Collusion

22. _____ is a fee paid on borrowed assets. It is the price paid for the use of borrowed money , or, money earned by deposited funds .Assets that are sometimes lent with _____ include money, shares, consumer goods through hire purchase, major assets such as aircraft, and even entire factories in finance lease arrangements. The _____ is calculated upon the value of the assets in the same manner as upon money.
   a. Interest
   b. AIG
   c. Insolvency
   d. ABC Television Network

23. _____ is the value on a given date of a future payment or series of future payments, discounted to reflect the time value of money and other factors such as investment risk. _____ calculations are widely used in business and economics to provide a means to compare cash flows at different times on a meaningful 'like to like' basis.

The most commonly applied model of the time value of money is compound interest.

   a. Net present value
   b. Future value
   c. 3M Company
   d. Present value

24. In mathematics _____s are numbers or other things that get multiplied. In particular, see:

   - Factorization, the decomposition of an object into a product of other objects
   - Integer factorization, the process of breaking down a composite number into smaller non-trivial divisors
   - A coefficient
   - A divisor of a particular number, or of an element of a monoid
   - A von Neumann algebra with a trivial center

In statistics

   - _____ analysis is the study of how _____s or certain variables affect variables.

Chapter 18. Allocation of Support Activity Costs and Joint Costs

In technology:

- Human _____s, a profession that focuses on how people interact with products, tools, or procedures
- 'Functionality, Application domain, Conditions, Technology, Objects and Responsibility;', In object-oriented programming

In computer science and information technology:

- Authentication _____, a piece of information used to verify a person's identity for security purposes
- _____, a Unix command for numbers factorization
- _____ (programming language), an experimental Forth-like programming language

In television:

- The O'Reilly _____, an American talk show hosted by Bill O'Reilly on Fox News.
- The Krypton _____, a British game show hosted by Gordon Burns, formally on ITV. Also had an American version.

a. Valuation	b. The Goodyear Tire ' Rubber Company
c. Merck ' Co., Inc.	d. Factor

25. Discounting is a financial mechanism in which a debtor obtains the right to delay payments to a creditor, for a defined period of time, in exchange for a charge or fee. Essentially, the party that owes money in the present purchases the right to delay the payment until some future date. The _____, or charge, is simply the difference between the original amount owed in the present and the amount that has to be paid in the future to settle the debt.

a. Discounting	b. Risk aversion
c. Discount	d. Discount factor

26. The _____ is an interest rate a central bank charges depository institutions that borrow reserves from it.

The term _____ has two meanings:

- the same as interest rate; the term 'discount' does not refer to the meaning of the word, but to the purpose of using the quantity, such as computations of present value, e.g. net present value or discounted cash flow

- the annual effective _____, which is the annual interest divided by the capital including that interest; this rate is lower than the interest rate; it corresponds to using the value after a year as the nominal value, and seeing the initial value as the nominal value minus a discount; it is used for Treasury Bills and similar financial instruments

The annual effective _____ is the annual interest divided by the capital including that interest, which is the interest rate divided by 100% plus the interest rate. It is the annual discount factor to be applied to the future cash flow, to find the discount, subtracted from a future value to find the value one year earlier.

For example, suppose there is a government bond that sells for $95 and pays $100 in a year's time.

a. Convertible bond
b. Process time
c. Municipal bond
d. Discount rate

27. The term _____ is used in finance theory to refer to any terminating stream of fixed payments over a specified period of time. This usage is most commonly seen in academic discussions of finance, usually in connection with the valuation of the stream of payments, taking into account time value of money concepts such as interest rate and future value.

Examples of these are regular deposits to a savings account, monthly home mortgage payments and monthly insurance payments.

a. Annuity
b. Appropriation
c. Intangible
d. Improvement

28. The _____ is a performance management tool which began as a concept for measuring whether the smaller-scale operational activities of a company are aligned with its larger-scale objectives in terms of vision and strategy.

By focusing not only on financial outcomes but also on the operational, marketing and developmental inputs to these, the _____ helps provide a more comprehensive view of a business, which in turn helps organizations act in their best long-term interests. This tool is also being used to address business response to climate change and greenhouse gas emissions.

a. Balanced scorecard
b. Trustee
c. Management by objectives
d. Best practice

29. _____ is an area of engineering practice concerned with the 'application of scientific principles and techniques to problems of cost estimating, cost control, business planning and management science, profitability analysis, project management, and planning and scheduling.'

Key objectives of _____ are to arrive at accurate cost estimates and to avoid cost overruns. The broad array of _____ topics represent the intersection of the fields of project management, business management, and engineering. Most people have a limited view of what engineering encompasses.

a. BNSF Railway
b. BMC Software, Inc.
c. 3M Company
d. Cost engineering

30. _____ is the calculated approximation of a result which is usable even if input data may be incomplete or uncertain.

In statistics, see _____ theory, estimator.

In mathematics, approximation or _____ typically means finding upper or lower bounds of a quantity that cannot readily be computed precisely and is also an educated guess .

a. Estimation b. ABC Television Network
c. AMEX d. AIG

Chapter 1
1. b   2. d   3. a   4. c   5. d   6. d   7. c   8. d   9. a   10. a
11. d   12. d   13. a   14. a   15. a   16. d   17. b   18. c   19. c   20. a
21. a   22. a   23. b   24. d   25. d   26. d   27. d   28. d   29. a   30. d
31. b   32. d   33. d   34. d   35. d   36. d   37. a   38. d   39. a   40. d
41. d   42. d   43. d   44. d   45. c   46. a

Chapter 2
1. d   2. d   3. d   4. d   5. c   6. d   7. d   8. d   9. d   10. b
11. b   12. d   13. c   14. d   15. d   16. a   17. c   18. d   19. d   20. d
21. d   22. d   23. a   24. c   25. d   26. a   27. c   28. a   29. c   30. b
31. c   32. a

Chapter 3
1. b   2. d   3. b   4. b   5. d   6. d   7. b   8. d   9. d   10. b
11. c   12. d   13. d   14. b   15. d   16. d   17. c   18. c   19. d   20. d
21. d   22. a   23. d   24. c   25. b   26. d   27. d

Chapter 4
1. a   2. c   3. d   4. d   5. d   6. a   7. b   8. b   9. d   10. d
11. d   12. d   13. d

Chapter 5
1. c   2. d   3. d   4. c   5. d   6. a   7. d   8. d   9. a   10. d
11. d   12. b   13. d   14. d   15. a   16. c   17. a

Chapter 6
1. a   2. d   3. a   4. c   5. a   6. d   7. b   8. d   9. c   10. a
11. d   12. c   13. d   14. d   15. d   16. c   17. d   18. d   19. d   20. d
21. c   22. c   23. a   24. d   25. a   26. c   27. d   28. b   29. a

Chapter 7
1. a   2. d   3. c   4. b   5. c   6. b   7. a   8. d   9. b   10. a
11. d   12. d   13. d   14. a   15. c   16. d   17. d   18. c   19. a   20. d
21. a   22. b

Chapter 8
1. a   2. a   3. a   4. d   5. a   6. d   7. a   8. b   9. a   10. b
11. b   12. d   13. d   14. c   15. a   16. c   17. b   18. d   19. a   20. b
21. d   22. d   23. d   24. b   25. d   26. b   27. d

Chapter 9
1. d   2. c   3. b   4. d   5. b   6. d   7. b   8. c   9. a   10. d
11. d   12. c   13. b   14. d   15. b   16. c   17. c   18. a   19. d   20. c
21. d   22. d   23. d   24. d   25. b   26. d   27. d   28. b   29. d   30. d
31. b   32. c   33. b   34. a

ANSWER KEY

Chapter 10
1. d	2. c	3. d	4. c	5. c	6. d	7. c	8. d	9. d	10. a
11. d	12. d	13. a	14. b	15. a	16. d	17. c	18. a	19. d	20. b
21. d	22. a	23. b	24. d	25. a	26. b	27. d	28. d	29. d	30. d
31. d	32. d	33. d	34. d	35. a	36. d	37. d	38. d	39. d	40. b
41. d	42. a	43. c	44. c	45. a	46. d	47. d	48. d		

Chapter 11
| 1. c | 2. d | 3. d | 4. c | 5. d | 6. c | 7. b | 8. d | 9. d | 10. d |
| 11. a | 12. d | 13. b | 14. d | 15. b | 16. b | 17. c | 18. d | 19. a | |

Chapter 12
1. d	2. d	3. c	4. c	5. d	6. c	7. a	8. d	9. b	10. d
11. b	12. d	13. d	14. d	15. a	16. d	17. a	18. c	19. d	20. d
21. a	22. b	23. d	24. d	25. c	26. c				

Chapter 13
1. c	2. d	3. b	4. a	5. d	6. b	7. b	8. d	9. d	10. a
11. d	12. b	13. d	14. d	15. d	16. b	17. d	18. a	19. d	20. b
21. d	22. d	23. d	24. d	25. b	26. d	27. a	28. d	29. c	30. b
31. d	32. d	33. a	34. c	35. d	36. d	37. b	38. d	39. c	40. d
41. b	42. c	43. d	44. d	45. b	46. c	47. d	48. b	49. d	50. b
51. a	52. c	53. d	54. b						

Chapter 14
1. a	2. d	3. d	4. c	5. b	6. d	7. b	8. b	9. c	10. b
11. d	12. d	13. d	14. a	15. c	16. a	17. c	18. d	19. c	20. d
21. a	22. c	23. a	24. d	25. b	26. d	27. a	28. b	29. b	30. c
31. b	32. c	33. c	34. b	35. d	36. d	37. d	38. a	39. d	40. d
41. d									

Chapter 15
1. b	2. d	3. d	4. d	5. d	6. d	7. c	8. a	9. a	10. a
11. d	12. a	13. a	14. d	15. d	16. a	17. c	18. d	19. c	20. a
21. d	22. c	23. d	24. c	25. a	26. a	27. d	28. d	29. d	30. d
31. d	32. c	33. c	34. b	35. c	36. a	37. c	38. b	39. a	40. b
41. c									

Chapter 16
1. c	2. a	3. b	4. a	5. d	6. d	7. d	8. d	9. b	10. a
11. d	12. d	13. c	14. b	15. c	16. b	17. c	18. d	19. d	20. d
21. d	22. a	23. d	24. d	25. d	26. a	27. c	28. d	29. d	30. c
31. a	32. b	33. a	34. d	35. d	36. c	37. d	38. d	39. d	40. d
41. c	42. d	43. b	44. c	45. a	46. a	47. c	48. c	49. d	

Chapter 17

| 1. b | 2. c | 3. a | 4. c | 5. b | 6. d | 7. c | 8. d | 9. d | 10. d |
| 11. d | 12. d | 13. a | 14. d | 15. c | 16. d | 17. c | | | |

Chapter 18

1. b	2. c	3. d	4. d	5. d	6. b	7. d	8. c	9. c	10. d
11. d	12. d	13. c	14. b	15. d	16. b	17. a	18. a	19. a	20. d
21. a	22. a	23. d	24. d	25. c	26. d	27. a	28. a	29. d	30. a